Finally, The TRUTH About HEALTH

The 5 Keys to health that promote a longer, happier and healthier life.

by

Dr. Bill F. Puglisi, D.C., C.C.W.P.

authorHOUSE

AuthorHouse™
1663 Liberty Drive, Suite 200
Bloomington, IN 47403
www.authorhouse.com
Phone: 1-800-839-8640

© 2008 Dr. Bill F. Puglisi, D.C., C.C.W.P.. All rights reserved.

No part of this book may be reproduced, stored in a retrieval system, or transmitted by any means without the written permission of the author.

First published by AuthorHouse 3/4/2008

ISBN: 978-1-4343-5615-4 (sc)

Library of Congress Control Number: 2007909730

Printed in the United States of America
Bloomington, Indiana

This book is printed on acid-free paper.

Elite Family Wellness Center
195 U.S. Highway 46 West
Totowa, NJ 07512
www.elitefamilywellness.com

Dedication is due...

This book is dedicated to Dr. Edward F. Karas, D.C., who literally saved my life when no other doctor could. But that was the small part. He also gave me a life. The miracles I saw him perform with the people suffering in his office, and also the wonderful personality he had, left an everlasting impression. There was genuine sincerity in his heart, and the pure love that he was made of made me want to be like him. He is the reason why I am alive today, he is the reason why I became a doctor, and he is why I wrote this book. I'm sorry I'm not half the man that you were on this earth, but I'm blessed and thankful that a tiny fraction of what you were, did rub off on me.

This book is also dedicated to the other wonderful people who have also influenced my life.

To Dr. Virgil Strang, Professor at Palmer College, in Iowa, whose many private talks with me showed me "The Big Idea" and what it really meant, and what it could really mean, if only a few more doctors, a few more patients, and a few more government officials, could just take the ball and run with it. Within one lifetime the whole world could be changed.

To Dr. C.J. Mertz, a chiropractor, a teacher, a mentor, and even though only an acquaintance for the past six years, a friend. The four days we spent in Texas will be four days that I will never forget. He showed me that any adversity can be overcome if you know what you are doing is the right thing, and you have a "passion" for doing what is right.

To Michael Massotto, another mentor and a friend, you stayed with me through thick and thin, and always stuck to your convictions. Most of what I learned from you, did not come from the words that you said, but from the example that you set. A clear mind, a clear vision, a healthy lifestyle, and a relentless pursuit of your dreams and goals... If half the world led a life summed-up by that sentence, the other half of the world would surely have to sit up and take notice. You led by example, and that is the best way to teach others. Thank you for simply being you.

To Dr. James L. Chestnut B.Ed, MSc., D.C., who taught me to be a student of the truth, not only for myself, but for the good of all the others around me, and to share that truth with others, freely. You also instilled in me that my studying and research into the truth about health will never, ever, ever, (ever) end. A lot of what is contained in this book is directly from your teachings. Thank you.

Finally, this book is dedicated to the many patients that I have had the privilege to meet and to help over the past 24 years. I have never looked at what I do as a business. That's probably why I am not a millionaire. But like the line at the end of the Jimmy Stewart movie *"It's a Wonderful Life"* says... *"No man is poor who has friends"*. I consider each and every one of the people I have treated over the years as my friends. That is thousands of people, and that makes me one of the richest men on the face of the earth. I hope my heart has touched you a little, just as yours has touched mine.

To the many medical doctors, chiropractors, and other health care professionals I've met over the years, and to the many more that I haven't ...
STOP THE NONSENSE!

Table of Contents

Chapter 1 –   A little bit of truth…   1

     "The truth goes through three stages. First it is ridiculed, then it is violently opposed, then finally, it is accepted as truth"

Chapter 2 –   Is there more to me than just me?   10

     "prayer is not asking, it is admission of weakness, so in prayer it is better to have a heart without words, than words without a heart."

Chapter 3 –   Before the "Do's" we need to learn the Why's and "How's"   20

     "You don't have to go College to become an idiot, you can do that on your own, but college helps"

Chapter 4 –   Genetics 101   34

     "It is not the answer that enlightens, but the question"

Chapter 5 –   Stress, or Distress?   40

     "We can easily forgive a child who is afraid of the dark, the real tragedy is when adults are afraid of the light"

Chapter 6 –   Natural Health Care 101   58

     "First they laugh at you, then they ridicule you, then they beat you, then you win!"

Chapter 7 –   But what do I eat? The best foods, the worst foods   86

     "Give a man a fish and you feed him for a day, teach a man to fish and feed him for a lifetime"

Chapter 8 – Give it a rest… 114

"Work when there is work to do. Rest when you are tired. One thing done in peace is better than ten things done in panic…"

Chapter 9 – Exercise, the final "Ingredient" 122

"When stressed, anxious, nervous, worried, mad, distraught, or in despair, go for a walk…"

Chapter 10 – Putting it together…the lifetime wellness plan 132

"Where there is peace and meditation there is neither anxiety nor doubt…"

Chapter 10b – Is that all there is? 139

"People have a hard time letting go of their suffering; out of fear of the unknown they prefer suffering, that is familiar"

Chapter 1
A little bit of truth...

"The truth goes through three stages. First it is ridiculed, then it is violently opposed, then finally, it is accepted as self evident."

Schoepenhouer

"The truth will set you free, but first it will make you mad..."

...Some of the names have not been changed because the innocent need not be protected, and the guilty need to atone for their actions...

I was born in 1957, in a city called Paterson, in New Jersey. It was once known as the 'Silk City' for its booming silk industry. It is also the birthplace of the great comedian Lou Costello, (my real claim to fame).

I'm just an average person like most of you who are reading this book. So why am I writing this book? What does an average person have to tell all the other average people and above average people out there? Well, as it turns out, a lot.

Through my 24 years of private practice, and the continuing education I've received, and the continuous research that I have done, my hunger and thirst for the truth about health has led me to many basic discoveries that I know to be true without a doubt. Yet I have also discovered that about 90 % of the people I meet don't know these basic truths, not even the so-called experts. In fact some of the *"experts"* that I have found, are one of the groups that seem to know the least. You will see me asking *"why"* very often throughout this book. I will then make my best and most honest attempt to answer the ***whys*** with facts that I hope will make sense. When I first started finding out the truth, some of my first "whys" were: Why doesn't the general public know this? Why don't the so-called experts even know this? As is the usual case, when you delve deep into a very specific subject, you start to uncover facts and answers that are somewhat surprising. One of the things I've found is that one of the many reasons the general public does not know the truth about health is that many of those self-proclaimed experts actually *do* know, but they do not want the public to know, because of the financial

1

interest they may have in keeping these truths a secret. For example, some people don't even know this simple truth, (although I think most people are starting to learn this one by now):

Big Drug companies have a product to sell. If you get right down to it they only have one product to sell: drugs. If they do not sell drugs then they go out of business. Their main responsibility is to stay in business, and to make money for their stockholders, their employees, and themselves. Their purpose is NOT to make people healthier, or cure disease. Well, drug companies are among the most profitable businesses on earth, each making many billions and even trillions of dollars each and every year! All by just selling their one product, drugs. Please follow this reasoning very carefully: Do drug companies sell most of their drugs to healthy people or to sick people? The obvious answer is that almost all drugs are sold to "sick" people, or at least to people who think they are "sick." Why would the drug companies want to cure any disease? Well, they don't. And they won't. No matter what they tell you, drug companies are only in the business of selling drugs, and most all of the drugs are for symptoms that people have who believe they are sick. Period! The marketing of all drugs from all drug companies is centered on keeping you sick or making you think you are sick. This will never change, unless the drug company decides to give up making drugs and develop a new and different product to sell. Sometimes you can't fight City Hall. This is especially true when City Hall is owned by the drug companies.

I promise that I will not spend the rest of this book bashing drug companies, but you should know a few undeniable facts that I have uncovered in my years of study. I will give you the facts to support my statements, and then leave it at that. This book is mainly about how to live a longer, happier, healthier life (and a little about me and my life story), neither of which has anything to do with drugs or drug companies. Before we begin, here are a few undeniable facts about drug companies:

The leading drug companies can gross TRILLIONS of dollars in sales each year. That's right. More than millions, more than billions, and they spend more than 15% of their income on marketing and advertising, which came to roughly 23 billion dollars in 2004 for some of the successful drug companies. It gets higher every year. They spend less than this, in fact less than 9%, in research and development, and even less on after market safety programs and follow-up. With regard to safety, remember that the FDA is supposed to "approve" of a drug before it goes to market. But guess who owns the FDA? Even though this is supposed to be a government administration that is in place to protect the public, nothing could be further from the truth. Most of the top officials on the FDA are former drug company executives. Once they have finished their stint serving on the FDA, they go back and work for the drug companies. This is not even that big of a secret. You can go look it up as a matter of public record. What do you think the FDA does when a drug comes up for approval? Lots of scientific research, right? Well in fact, they usually do <u>no research at all</u>. They review the research the drug company gives them that the drug company did on their own drug! And so common sense would tell you what these former/future drug company executives are going to say about the safety of the new drug right?

This is the reason for the drug Vioxx (rofecoxib). This is the reason for Fen-fen. This is the reason why almost 80% of drugs on the market today will eventually be pulled off the market and deemed unsafe or ineffective. They almost always are. I could write an entire book on this very scary but very true problem in our society, and maybe I will, but why beat a dead horse as they say. There are literally dozens of great books that have already been written on this subject. So I will refer you to those books for now, some of them are listed at the end of this book.

One final note to sum up the drug topic for now; EVERY drug has an LD-50 listed in the PDR (Physicians Desk Reference). Even over the counter drugs. An LD-50 means "Lethal-dose-50%," which means that every drug, even aspirin and Tylenol, has a specific dose, or amount, that when given to a population of people will kill 50% of that population. Why is it expressed this way? Because if a drug has an LD-50, then automatically the drug also has an LD-100! That means that Lipator, Nexxium, and EVERY drug, even aspirin and Tylenol, have a specific amount or dose, that when given to a population of people, will kill ALL the population of those people. More simply put, any drug can be taken in such an amount that it will kill you, every time! It's the same thing, but they would not tell it to you in those terms. See, EVERY drug is a deadly toxic chemical by definition. They are just prescribed in sub-lethal doses so you don't die right away. You just stay sick so you can continue to purchase more drugs.

Just keep them sick and then sell them stuff for the symptoms of their sickness. A pretty clever marketing strategy, don't you think? Please ask yourself this question: How can taking a sub-lethal dose of a known deadly toxic chemical ever produce health in my body? Now try to answer that question from a common sense point of view. See, the truth, once revealed, usually makes sense all of a sudden, making it easier to accept. It is sometimes hard to discover the truth; but the *hardest* part is accepting the truth *as truth*, and getting the old big lie, or misinformation, out of your head so you can put the seemingly new, truthful information in. Only then will it begin to make sense and really become true for you, even though it was always true all the time. Think of Hitler and Nazi Germany. If you tell a big enough lie to a lot of people, often enough, they will come to believe it as true, especially if they think you are some kind of an authority. Well, Hitler, and Nazi Germany, happens every day at some level or another, when it comes to general health information. That's one of the main reasons why I wrote this book. And that's why one of the most important and valuable things I could ever teach you, or anyone, is right here in the first chapter of this humble book.

Here it is. If anyone gives you information related to health, and it is at all different from what I say in this book, always ask him or her, **"Where did you read that, and can I get a copy?"** Now, I'm not saying that to be egotistical. I am probably not the single most knowledgeable person in the whole world on the topic of health, but I have reviewed the research and I do know what is true. You see, there is a lot of bad health information out there in the general public. Most of that bad information is carefully placed out there by those people who have an agenda, usually a product to sell. I don't have a product to sell. Many people write health and diet books, and then at the end of their book they tell you where you can buy their line of vitamins. Many people write exercise books and then at the end tell you where you can buy their special exercise equipment, and on, and on, and on. Many doctors tell you that you need surgery, and then say; "by the way, I happen to do that surgery." Yet more than 40% of all surgeries for any condition, almost 200,000 per year just in the U.S. are later found to be unnecessary by experts who review the cases. Please be very, very wary and skeptical of people who tell you what you need in order to be healthy. They are normally the people who also just happen to provide the exact product that they say you need. It's usually just marketing. I do not have a product to sell you at the end of this book that promises to be the one thing you need to make you healthy. THERE IS NO ONE PRODUCT THAT EXISTS ANYWHERE THAT WILL GUARANTEE TO MAKE YOU HEALTHY.

The truth about health is that health is a process, health is a journey, and health is achievable.

After reading this book you will be armed with facts about health that I know to be true based on the current scientific research. Almost none of this book contains any information on health that is my opinion, or someone's theory, with the exception of a few statements made in the first two chapters only. Even the first two chapters include only facts as I see them, but I don't have 100% scientific proof for some of the information. Otherwise, 99.9% of the rest of this book contains facts that are the facts, fully backed by mainstream research. Remember again, if you see or hear anything that seems different, check the sources of that information. Question the reason why someone would say something different. Check their hidden agenda. Always ask them *"Where did you read that and can I get a copy?"* I wish I could take credit for that statement, but I learned it from Dr. James L. Chestnut B.Ed., MSc., D.C., one of the smartest men on the planet when it comes to knowing the truth about health. Once you are armed with the truth about health that is contained in this book, you can use these undeniable facts to start to make healthy lifestyle choices. This is the best starting point for your task of sorting through all the muck and mire of health information.

So much has been written about health, wellness, and fitness that is just plain wrong. I am convinced that many of you who are sincerely interested in your health are right now doing things for your health that you think are good for you, but are actually very unhealthy. But it's not your fault. You have been told that it is healthy to do certain things by the government and by the big farming and agricultural business that have their agendas. You have been told by self-proclaimed experts on infomercials that have a product to sell you. You have been told by magazine articles, which not only have a product to sell you but are almost totally controlled by the pharmaceutical industry, because it's the drug companies that do the most advertising and pay the most for advertising space in their magazine. They don't want to bite the hand that feeds them. The same goes for the newspaper and the news on TV. Drug companies pay them all millions of dollars to influence the content of their media. So now that you have been brainwashed by them, it seems like a no-brainer to consume conventional milk and dairy products or whole-wheat Wonder Bread, and think that they are healthy, instead of the dirty disgusting poison that they really are. Oh no! Did I just say that? I'm sure more than half of you are very upset right now, especially if you are a dairy farmer or work for the Wonder Bread Company. You probably want to throw away this book and wish you never bought it. I promise you in later chapters I will show you the undeniable facts that prove these are not healthy foods. Remember, I am only including facts that I know to be true based on the current scientific research. I'll show you these facts and point you to many scientific resources so that you can check it out for yourself. I mention them now because they are among the most controversial of the many deadly foods that are passed off as healthy foods, and I want you to be able to keep an objective mind when I discuss these topics. I swear I wouldn't say it if I didn't know for sure that it was true, or if I could not back it up with acceptable scientific research. Please trust me for now. The point here is that I will soon be discussing topics like this in detail and I don't want you to be upset or blow off the information as false, just because you believed differently up until now. Before I can discuss these and other topics I have to be sure you have an open and objective attitude toward these topics and are willing to hear the truth, and then be willing to change your opinion.

Previously I stated that it is sometimes hard to uncover the truth, but it is even harder to accept the truth *as truth*, especially if you have believed the lie for generations, as taught to you by your loving parents, your concerned school teacher, your caring medical doctor, your friends and your next-door neighbor. Well, I'm sure all their hearts were in the right place, but did you ask them *"Where did you read that and can I get a copy?"* If not, go back and do it. They deserve to know the truth too. In fact, I educate a lot of medical doctors, some of whom even become my patients once I show them their own medical research that backs up everything I do and say. So please hold on for now and keep reading, and hopefully it will all come together and make sense to you. Once again, the ultimate goal of this book is to simply arm you with truthful scientific information about health, so that you can then use the facts to make better decisions regarding your health. That's all. It's strong and it's powerful information that can and will change your life. It may even save your life like it did mine. But once finished you can take it or leave it. It's up to you. It's all about choice. You can choose to change your life for the better, or choose to continue to commit suicide by your present lifestyle choices, it's up to you.

You see, there are only three kinds of people in the world:
One: Those who need and want help;
Two: Those who need help and don't know it;
Three: Those who don't want any help.

Whichever group you fit into, that's o.k. I promise that I still love you and care about you. I won't force you to do anything that you don't want to do. I can only help people in those first two groups. In fact, if you sincerely say you don't want to change your present lifestyle choices for a healthier life, I'll be the first one to tell you that it's o.k. not to. I'm not an evangelical preacher. Whatever you decide to do is alright for you and o.k. with me. See, choosing to change for the wrong reason is often just as bad as doing the wrong things in the first place. You must, however, accept the consequences of your actions, or inactions. So long as you can live with yourself and sleep well at night, then I can live with you too.

I make these statements here because I do care; I care very much about the health of the planet that I live on, and the people who live on it with me. But not enough to stress anyone or myself to change their decision-making for the wrong reasons. That, in itself, is a stress. For example, if you go on a diet to lose weight out of fear of having a heart attack, the fact is you will most likely have a heart attack. If you try to stop smoking out of fear that you may develop a lung disease, then you most likely will develop a lung disease. This is true because of another little-known fact that all people should know. The stress that fear and anxiety causes has just as strong a negative effect on the health of your body as does being overweight or as smoking. Stress is by far the number one cause of heart attacks, far beyond that of being overweight or smoking. Of course I'm not saying that either obesity or smoking is in any way good for you. It is a known fact that smoking is directly related to lung disease, and being overweight is directly related to heart conditions. The change in the physiology of your body that stress causes however, is by far a bigger biomarker for heart disease than any of the risk factors that you are all familiar with. So much so that soon you will see I have dedicated an entire chapter of the book toward understanding stress and how it affects your physical condition.

Know for now that going on a diet out of fear will never work. Going on a diet because I said so will also never work. As a matter of fact, going on a diet will never work period. That's because there is fear, denial, deprivation and anxiety associated with almost every diet. That's all negative. And the stress that those negative emotions cause, can and often do result in just as much damage to your body as being overweight. More facts about this will be discussed later in the chapter on stress. For now the point is, when you read something here, keep an open mind and stay objective, please. Try to remember that it is well researched information that is documented by scientific medical studies. Remember that I have no product to sell you, or any other hidden agenda. Remember that I use all this information for myself, my family, and the patients in my practice. There simply is no ulterior motive other than to disclose true health information that you can use to make better health-related decisions for you and your family.

Try not to struggle or stress over any of the information. If you're not sure about something, just do more research on it yourself. Contact me and I will be glad to give you scientific studies to start your investigations.

Many of them that I will be quoting in this book are good places to start.

Also, please keep an open HEART, as well as an open mind. Don't kill the messenger. Read carefully all of the facts and information presented here. Understand it. Digest it. Make it part of you, for your own sake. And above all, once it makes sense to you and you know it to be right in your heart, mind, and soul, PLEASE SHARE IT with others as well, so they may benefit too. But don't force it on them. Don't argue with them. Once you know that you're right, then you are right! Please don't feel the need to defend yourself and your point of view at all costs, or you will get to the point where you are stressed. And as you will learn, stress is unhealthy. Stress kills. As in all aspects of life, it's always a choice. Make friends with everyone you meet, even those with unhealthy lifestyles. Choose to live happy and healthy lives. (But only if you really *want* to.) And the best way to teach them is by example anyway. Test out what you learn here on yourself. Try it my way for about 90-100 days in a row. Keep notes on any changes and on how you feel in general. Then go back to the old way you did things for a short while. If you don't notice any difference let me know. I will be happy to refund the money you paid for this book if you don't feel any better after trying it my way. But if you do notice a difference, then go back to making your health choices the way this book describes. Become as healthy and as happy as you can become; then it will be easy to teach others. They will learn by your example. And if they don't, that's o.k. because even if you do not convert one single person into a healthier lifestyle, you still have gained a more optimum level of health for yourself than you have ever had before, and that can't be all bad, could it?

I'm almost done rambling in this first chapter. My final suggestion is that you read this entire book like a story, from beginning to end, in order, without skipping around. At that point you'll know what you know and remember what you remember. Then go back and read it again, taking notes on the parts that you need to know but did not remember. Also take notes on the parts that you may still have some resistance to believing are really true, so you can do more reading on those topics and then you can be convinced about the truth of a statement one way or the other. Hey, you may even find something that is new and/or different from what I've stated, although I doubt it. Someone famous once said: *"the biggest mistake you could ever make is to always be right."* No matter what the results are from reading this book twice and then doing some further reading about related topics, at least one way or the other you will know the truth, and that's all that really counts anyway. I have people send me scientific research studies all the time for me to review and critique, (That's where I got some of the information in this book, but please don't tell them that).

The truth about health is that health is a formula that is within your grasp to apply. Health is purely a choice.

If you use this book in the way I just described I know that you will be almost *bullet-proof* when confronted by someone who disagrees with these facts and tries to argue with you. Even your medical doctor won't be able to push you around anymore. And that my good friends could save your life. Good luck, have fun and remember... don't stress...

Chapter 2

Is there more to you than just you? Or: Belief- Faith- Science?

"Prayer is <u>not asking</u>, <u>it is admission</u> of one's weakness, and so it is better in prayer to have a heart without words, than words without a heart."
Gandhi

Back to Paterson, New Jersey.

My experience in the health care system started young. As a patient who was very sick. I was born healthy and normal. But like all too many infants these days, after a vaccination I developed serious symptoms. In my case it was the polio vaccine, and the symptoms were respiratory. I got worse and worse and my degenerating condition was finally diagnosed as asthma, along with severe allergies. The pediatrician was smart enough to never let me be vaccinated again. This may have been because my mother was his receptionist and assistant. He had been taking care of me since the day I was born. These days a large number of pediatricians do not vaccinate their own children. (They are too smart for that. But they continue to vaccinate your children, mostly due to money and peer pressure). I have an extensive library of books and scientific articles all documenting the common dangers of most vaccines. The topic is so controversial and complicated that it would take another entire book to cover it properly. Even though the evidence is overwhelming that they are not necessary in most cases, and contain deadly toxic chemicals that cause disease. There are at least a hundred books that scientifically document their dangers, and the lies that the drug companies and the government tell the public about them. I urge you very strongly to do the research on these deadly poisons, and come to your own conclusions. I apologize that I don't have the space here to convince you now.

Over the next eighteen months or so my condition got so bad that the doctor referred me out to a specialist in New York City. I had so many serious asthma attacks that I was in the emergency room at least 10 times, and was usually admitted into the hospital, at least overnight. My parents took me from "expert" to "expert," all coming up with treatments and medications that failed horribly. Finally, the last time I was taken to the hospital emergency room, they determined that my lung had collapsed. For those of you who don't know about asthma, it is a reaction of your respiratory system that causes constriction of the bronchioles, the tubes that allow air to pass into your lungs. This makes breathing very difficult. Well, when you can't breathe already, and then your lung deflates leaving you with only one, the scenario is not very good. My whole body turned blue, a condition called cyanosis, due to the lack of oxygen in my blood. The wise and honest doctors at the hospital admitted that there was nothing they could do for me. They had already tried everything they could possibly do for almost two years with no positive results. They told my parents that I could stay there, or they could take me home to die, which would save my parents some hospital bills. (I told you they were wise and honest.) My parents decided to take me home. I was given my "Last Rights" by a priest in the hospital. Once at home, I was given my Last Rights again, this time by the family priest. Last Rights are something that Catholic families do, basically to make sure you get into heaven without too many delays. It kind of ties up loose ends here on earth. This is especially important for very old and very young people who are dying. This is something that big, old-fashioned Italian families do. I could write a whole book on what big old-fashioned Italian families do. I will save that story for another time, however.

One other thing that big, old-fashioned Italian families do is to let everyone know that someone in the family is dying. Everyone in the family, and all the Italian friends of everyone in the family, then come to visit the family with the dying family member. Got all that so far? Everyone came and said a prayer, and of course brought some food. Well, one of the people who came to visit me for the last time was my Aunt Mary. Aunt Mary brought her Italian next-door neighbor and friend, Josephine, of course. She came to pray and bring some food. With them came Eddie, Josephine's young son. Eddie was a chiropractor, just out of school for a few years. Wait! Don't close the book yet!

The time was back in 1960-1961 when this all happened (yea I'm THAT old). Back then, and even sometimes today, chiropractic care was thought of as only for treating back pain. So when Doctor Eddie asked if he could check me out to see if there was anything he could do, my parents first rejected the idea. I would say they laughed at the idea, but that was not a time in their life when there was much laughter about anything. Their only son was dying. But after much explanation and education about what chiropractic care is really all about and what it could possibly do for a person, they reluctantly agreed. After all, I was going to die anyway according to all the medical "experts" from here to New York City and back. What harm could it do?

Doctor Eddie came into my room and saw a cyanotic child gasping for breath. He examined me, and found that there was a subluxation in my neck. A subluxation is a slight misalignment of a bone or joint out of place that causes an irritation to your spinal cord or nerve root. It is a very real and common occurrence… More on this later…

Well Doctor Eddie gently and carefully "adjusted" the bone in my neck back to where he thought is should be. The immediate result was that I took a gasp of breath, and fell asleep. It was the first time in years I was breathing silently. Everyone thought I was dead. It was the first time anyone could ever remember me sleeping that long, about 11-12 hours by most relatives account of the story. The miracle was the next day. I woke up, pink instead of blue. I never had another major asthma attack again. In fact with continued care from Doctor Eddie, I was able to eventually get rid of all signs of my asthma, my lung began working normally, and all signs of my allergies would soon disappear.

I even remember getting a dog when I was young. A dachshund named Inga. I also had a canary that my grandfather gave me. It was special because my grandfather raised canaries and parakeets in his cellar. This is another thing that many old-fashioned Italian families used to do. It was also special because I could never have a pet before. I could never go near a bird, cat, or dog without having an allergy attack. Doctor Eddie saved my life, literally. Which was a pretty good thing I suppose, but on the other hand there was no more praying or free food.

You would not be reading this book, because I would not be here to write it, if it were not for an unbelievable lucky sequence of events, leading up to a simple chiropractic adjustment of my spine. I'm sure the prayers and free food helped too.

Later my mother quit working for Dr. Schienfield, the medical doctor who delivered me and who tried to take care of my adverse vaccine reaction, and she went to work for Doctor Eddie instead. When I was between eight and nine years old my mom and I were in downtown Paterson New Jersey waiting at a bus stop, when who should walk by but Dr. Schienfield. He asked my mom who I was and she said, "It's my son, little Billy. Don't you remember him? (Don't ever call me "little Billy" or I will find you, and the meeting won't be pleasant.) The doctor actually argued with her that it couldn't be me, the boy with severe asthma, allergies, and the collapsed lung, because I could not have survived. He said I must be adopted. She not only swore it was me, but explained that it was a chiropractor who saved my life. Of course he laughed at that, and till this day my mother says that he left thinking I was adopted, and that my mom made up the story because she couldn't accept my death. Luckily I have my original birth certificate from Paterson General Hospital as proof. Who says one person can't make a difference in the lives of many? Dr Edward F. Karas, DC, sure did, for me and a lot of other people.

As years went by I heard this story being told many times. I didn't really know anything about chiropractic care back then. All I knew was that I saw a lot of people get better from a lot of ailments just from chiropractic treatment, without any drugs or surgery. Chiropractic care was just part of our life. All I knew was that every time I went to get a spinal adjustment, I felt better. I never went to a medical doctor for anything that I could remember, with the exception of when I broke my arm when I fell off of my friend Carmen L's back yard swing, and the time I was walking in the stream with my friend Joe Kosch, and cut my foot on a piece of glass and had to have stitches. Two visits to the medical doctor from the time I was three and a half to the time I was 13. Not for illnesses, but for emergency care only. In my mind medical doctors were for sick people, and I was never really sick. I learned very early on that if I got a cold or flu that it was o.k., I would get better all on my own eventually, without the help of drugs or doctors.

When I was 14 my parents got divorced, a sad and all-too-common occurrence these days. It was about that time that I started to attend high school, good ole' John F. Kennedy High School in good ole' Paterson, New Jersey. It was about that time that I also realized that I had an older sister. Actually I always knew I had an older sister, but we were five years apart, and did not have much interest in each others' lives until this point. Also, my sister Debbie was raised mostly by my mom and they spent most of their time with each other, and I was raised mostly by my dad and spent most of my time with him. Being a kid, I didn't think there was anything wrong with that because I never knew anything different. My dad and I did everything together. We went fishing almost every weekend from March until the lake would freeze over in December. We went rain or shine. Fishing was important to my dad and it became important to me too. I learned many lessons from those days out on the lake. I loved the outdoors and even became a Boy Scout for a few years. It seems my sister lead a different life when we were young. In fact she was different. She was beautiful. She was in the "in" crowd. She had lots of friends. When she was 16 she started taking singing lessons, dance lessons, acting lessons, and modeling lessons in New York City. By 17 she was modeling. She won a beauty contest down at the New Jersey shore... "Miss Keansburg." My mom was always with her on all these trips and me and my dad were somewhere else, fishing, car races, slot car racing, playing basketball. If not with him I was with my friend Joe K., fishing, car races, slot car racing, and playing basketball. That's almost all we did. I was different too. I was not beautiful. I was not in the "in" crowd. I had a very few but really good friends, but that was it. I was basically a loner.

My friend Joe and I also went to the movies a lot. Almost every Saturday Joe and I would go fishing down the park in the morning, then for 50 cents we would go to the noon movie at the Plaza Movie Theater. We would see two, yes two different movies, back to back with a whole bunch of shorts and cartoons in between. We were heart broken when the price went up to 75 cents. (I told you I was old.) We would get home after 4:00 in the afternoon. We were gone all day long on our bikes with just a pair of shorts, a t-shirt, and less than a dollar in our pockets. We sometimes rode our bikes for many miles to go fishing along the Passaic River, which wound through many towns nearby. No one ever worried about us or even knew where we were. After the movies we would hurry to get ready to go to the stock-car races in Middletown, New York, on Saturday nights, with Joe's uncle. A pretty full day. Out of the house from 6 a.m. until midnight. Sundays I would go to church with my grandmother Angie, and then go fishing again, this time with my dad. We would spend the day at the lake, sometimes from sunrise, until it got too dark to fish. In between I learned to swim at the lake. In fact my grammar school principal was the swimming teacher there. Mr. Glass from P.S. #5 in Paterson. He looked a lot like Bob Barker from "The Price is Right" game show, but not as nice. Everyone was afraid of him, I guess because he was the principal of the school. I had been in trouble more than once and ended up in his office at school a few times. I learned how to fish out of a boat at the lake too. I learned about camping and about nature at the lake. I grew up at the lake. When I was off from school during summer vacations I would be there almost every day. It was only a 25-minute drive from my house. It was about a two-hour bicycle ride. Yes, we even rode our bikes that far to go fishing. Please don't tell my parents because we had to cross some busy highways to get there.

Times have changed these days, although until very recently I continued to fish, go to car races, and raced cars myself.

When I started high school and my parents got divorced, things changed a little. I started to get to know my sister, slowly over the years. When she got married she asked me to be in her wedding. We used to go snowmobiling with her new husband in New York State. We got closer. When she had children I would baby-sit for her a lot. Funny how things change. Other than my own son, I am closer to her than any one else on the planet right now. Love is a powerful thing. I love everything about my sister now, and I love her children like they were my own. I would do anything for her, or her children, in the blink of an eye, without question.

I don't want to get too mushy, but I think love is the only thing really powerful enough to make someone actually want to change. That goes for love of the thought of being healthy, too. That's the only way you will ever make true stress-free changes and decisions toward a healthier lifestyle. Like I said before, if you change out of fear of a bad outcome, then the stress of that will affect you negatively. If you change just because I said so and it seems like a good thing to do, you may reach short-term goals, but it won't be permanent. You have to be in love with the idea. You have to love yourself and the people that are important in your life, enough to want to make the change in your life with all your heart, soul, and mind. You have to love the body that God has given you, and appreciate it enough to worship it as the temple of your spirit. That's the only way to make passing up the French fries and the ice cream an easy decision.

While we are on the subject of worshiping your body, I started this chapter with a quote from Gandhi about prayer. This is a touchy subject for most people. I promised that I would only present facts in this book. Facts that I could back up with scientific research. Believe it or not there is actually scientific evidence that human beings are much more than just their parts, or just their "physical" bodies. Most refer to this "greater than the sum" as the spiritual side of existence. Unfortunately when this subject comes up, people classify the discussion as religious, and say it is only belief and or faith, with no science. I am not going to have a long-winded religious discussion in this book. But I will present some facts here in this chapter, and some more facts in further chapters that do deserve at least some consideration, since they are related to the healing process and health in general. I won't claim that the following few paragraphs are 100% iron-clad facts, but I believe they are, and I believe strongly that when considering health, you should consider the following information.

First, *more than 98%* of all the people in the world believe that human beings have a spiritual side to their existence. Unfortunately because of cultural differences, language differences, and deep-rooted traditions, it sometimes seems that almost 98% of the people can't agree on exactly what the right story is. But the reason that they can't agree is really only because of those cultural, language, and traditional differences. When you come right down to it, they really do all agree on a basic premise, but they agree from a different point of view, based only on past experiences and what they were told to believe by their parents. All 98-plus percent still believe with all their heart, mind and soul, that there is a greater power, or energy in the universe, and we are somehow connected to that power. That's billions of people from all over the world, believing the same basic thing. Sophisticated and non-sophisticated people. Tribal and modernized people. Educated and non-educated people. Scientific and non-scientific people. In every culture of every people from every part of the globe there is this common belief. Global mass-hysteria? I don't think so, (and neither do the scientists.) So does it really matter what you call it just because you learned of it in a different language? Does it really matter that is was written in a different book by different people using different stories to make their point? I was raised as a Catholic from the day I was born. But if I was 4 years old, and I was at the airport with my family and was kidnapped by Muslims and brought to the Middle East, I may have grown up to be one of the people who crashed a plane into the World Trade Center buildings. And so might you have too. If you were raised Jewish until you were 9 years old, and then moved to China and while there your parents died and then you were raised by a Chinese family, you may now be a Buddhist. So who has his or her finger on the right religious belief? No one? Everyone? Fundamentally, I think they are all very similar. If more than 98% of the population of the earth believes that there is a greater power, from the uneducated to the most educated, don't you think it might be worth a little investigation on your part? Albert Einstein said, "There can be no science without religion." In some of his later interviews he also stated that at the most advanced levels of science and mathematics, the conclusions that are reached require a huge leap of faith, because there is no proof to many advanced mathematical theorems, and there is no proof to many of the accepted scientific claims. He has agreed with many of the world's leading scientists that these leaps of faith are much greater than those claimed by many of the world's leading religions. In fact, almost all the leading scientists of the world believe in some type of greater power or spiritual existence of some type, even though they can't agree on what it is.

From Einstein to Deepak Chopra, M.D., and everyone in between, people believe this, including some of the world's leading quantum physicists, who boldly claim that science does not contradict religion; it now actually supports many religious concepts and can all but prove them. Atheists are of the smallest minority compared to the population of the world. Can the entire world, including most of the scientific community, be wrong? Well, actually yes, they could be, but not likely. Logical thinking does lend itself to the notion that human beings are much more that just the sum of their parts. What causes the animation, growth, development, procreation, and the thinking process? I believe, along with some well-credentialed researchers, that it is the thinking process itself, the actual thought that controls it all. Quantum physics has proven that we are not really made out of matter; we are made out of energy. The smallest grain of sand, the largest mountain, and every human being is mostly empty space and energy. They have also proven that a thought is really just a wavelength of energy, not really different from any other forms of energy known to exist. But where is that process or thought in the recently deceased? They still have all the parts. They still have a connected brain and a connected body, full of all the necessary blood and organs that are still organized in such a way that, if we were just the sum of our parts, should still be working. Something is missing. You have something in you that the corpse does not have. I don't care what you call it. Call it soul, spirit, The Great Spirit, Creator, Life, life-force, life energy, God, mind, chi, Manitou, Thetan, Mother Nature, innate, innate intelligence, cosmic power, or "Mighty Joe the Wonder Puppy." It does not matter what you call it. Some quantum physicists, who are not absolutely sure, refer to the most basic form of existence as "information" and state that it is the actual "information energy" that cannot be created or destroyed, and that this "energy" is the basis of life. You don't have to call it anything at all, just know that it exists, and you are part of it, and it is part of you. That's all that really matters. I will discuss this a little more, later in the book, after we first learn how the human body really works and then how the human mind seems to works. (Good stuff is comin'...)

Before we can discuss the lifestyle choices we could be making to guarantee a longer, happier, healthier life, the best food to eat, the best exercise to do, the best sleep techniques, the best de-stressing techniques, and the best treatments and therapies, we first need to get to the basics of structure and function, and understand how it all works together. This may not be easy, but I will do my best to keep it simple and understandable. I do feel it is necessary that you have some understanding of the "**whys**" so that the recommendations in this book all make sense. If I suggest that you make a certain healthy choice just because I said so, and I did research to make sure it was healthy, that would not be enough to get you to change your thought process. There are lots of people out there telling you what to do. Half of them are wrong and half of them may even be right, but no one wants to be told what to do all the time. That would be stressful, and stress is unhealthy. You have to know why it is the right decision or choice, and you have to really want to do it with every fiber of your being, in order for it to be a stress-free choice that will stay with you forever. You have to love it. If anything you do for your health becomes too difficult to do over a long period of time, you simply won't stick with it, unless of course the end result happens to be something that is truly one of the top two or three priorities in your life. We need to understand why health *should be* one of the top priorities in our lives. It needs to be on our "to do" list every single day. The problem is that when you're not feeling "sick," health moves down on your list of priorities. You cannot be optimally healthy if you let this happen. We need to make this important but at the same time easy to do on a daily basis. If you don't change your belief system first, then this will be difficult. Once you understand *why*, then it may become important enough to keep it near the top of your list of priorities, and it will become easy. It will be just part of your daily routine like brushing your teeth.

Once again, in each chapter, I will try to give you the "whys." I will also give you the scientific references at the end of the book so you can check them out for yourself. Remember that it is important that you are confident that what you are reading in this book is the real deal. This book is the final word on the right things to do for the very basics of a healthy lifestyle. Take heed to my previous advice and read this book twice, and take notes the second time so you can do further investigation on your own to solidify the basic concepts presented here, in your mind. I can only tell you that they are true. That's not good enough. You have to know for sure that they are true. The only way to do that is by constant reading and education from the proper sources that have scientific research behind them. Your health and your life, and the life and health of your family, will be worth the effort.

The truth about health is that health comes from both the inside and the outside of your body. Health is balance.

I know that some of the things I said in this chapter may still sound like opinion. That's o.k. I think they may become more solid to you as you read on. If not, and you continue to disagree or have your own opinions about some of this chapter, that's o.k. too. But from this point on for the rest of the book, if you have a different opinion or disagree, THAT'S NOT O.K. The laws of health and wellness are about to be laid down. If you disagree with the following information then I would ask you *"Where did you read that and can I get a copy?!!"* (Thanks Dr. James)

Chapter 3
Before the "Do's"
We need to learn the "How's"
and the "Why's"

You don't have to go to college to become an idiot... That's a choice anyone can make for themselves at any time... but college helps!

Will Rodgers

Unfortunately I spent four years studying science in college; I had to go in order to get to where I wanted to be. Unfortunately I went to graduate school to become a doctor after that. I had to go there for the same reason. Fortunately I already knew exactly what I wanted to do in life before I graduated high school, which is where I learned most of life's really big lessons anyway. What I did not learn in high school, I learned from books written by experts that I was never exposed to in any school. I also learned by studying life naturally, and by learning from people who had already experienced life and seemed to have their act together. I learned the way all people used to learn before there was such a thing as a college. Then later, I realized that I went to college and just did "research" to confirm what I was learning was right. I also learned a lot by trial and error in 24 years of practice, treating people and getting them healthy, often when no one else could.

I went to Upsala College in East Orange, New Jersey. With the exception of one or two outstanding, world-class professors and a very few outstanding world-class students who became good friends, it was an inefficient use of four years of my life. Sorry, it sounds like I'm knocking them so hard. I'm not. It was actually one of the better colleges in the State at that time. I guess that doesn't say a lot for the rest of the colleges in general. It was just the time that bothered me the most. It seems that for all the money I paid and all the time I spent, college could have been so much more efficient. What I got out of college I could have learned in less than a year. Why did it take four years? Approximately two to three hours a week for 17 weeks, that's how much time you spend in a classroom to complete an average college course. That's 34 hours. Some are longer, some are shorter, but that's the average. If you're really a good student and spend another 34 hours outside that classroom studying for it, you probably passed it easily with at least a B, and maybe an A, if the professor liked you. Multiply those 68 hours by six classes a semester, that's 12 classes a year. Multiply that times four years and that's how long it takes to complete the average four-year college. If you don't feel like doing the math, here it is: 3200 hours; that's 134 days. Considering sleeping, eating, partying, and going to the bathroom, that's about 178 days. If you subtract weekends off, for more partying and more going to the bathroom, I figure the average person could complete a four-year college program in about 274 days if you attended six hours a day, five days a week. Well, maybe 275 days, but you get the point.

Time has become important to me lately. I don't really like inefficient use of time. I guess it's because I'm getting older. Days seem to go by faster and maybe I'm closer to the "end" end of my earthly existence than to the birth end of it. That's o.k.; it is the way of things. So be it. Time is a funny thing, though. It is a manmade invention of the mind, and doesn't really exist, at least not the way most people think about. It's similar to the concept of space. They kind of go together. Neither one is really conceivable. Both are human inventions of the mind to try to understand something that is not understandable in the truest sense. Try to get this concept in your head: When did time start? Close your eyes and go as far back into the history of time as you can imagine. Well, what was there before that? Time? What about before that? Time? Now close your eyes and go ahead into the future as far as you can think of; when does time end? What comes after that? Time! See? Do you have a clear picture in your head about what time really looks like? We think time is linear, but time is an ever-expanding continuous loop, with no beginning or end. If you try to rationalize it, you can't. You can't even conceive of a picture of it in your head. The only thing you can say about time is that it is "inconceptualizable"!

Now close your eyes and think about space. Take an element, an atom of that element. Break it down into its parts. Electrons, protons, neutrons, what about their parts? Photons, quarks, what's in between them? A huge amount of space. What is in between those subatomic particles? Space! What is between the particles that make up the particles? A huge amount of space! It's infinitely small. Go the other way now. What is beyond the stars? What is beyond the galaxies? Space. Go to the end of space and see what is beyond the end of space? Space! See?

Space is also infinitely large and never ending. Space, just like time, is also a continuous and ever-expanding loop. The only sure thing you can say about space is that it is inconceptualizable! That word I stole from Deepak Chopra, M.D., It's not in the dictionary. The point is that space and time cannot be imagined logically. They are not conceivable in the context of human existence and linear thought. One of the reasons is that we think we live in our own little world that has boundaries. We think we all have defined limits, so everything else must have limits too. But time and space are limitless, boundless, ever-existing and ever-expanding, with no beginning and no end. Science has proven that this phenomenon holds true for other thing in the universe, like energy, (and like us). Oh guess what, I didn't learn that in college either, but the study of quantum physics does prove it.

There are only four kinds of energy recognized by the scientific community of the world. Physicists recognize these as electro-magnetic energy, gravity, strong forces and weak forces. You are familiar with the first two I hope. Electro-magnetic energy makes up things like light, sound, magnetism, and radio waves. Gravity consists of the pulling forces between the earth, sun, and moon. Weak forces are basically defined as the forces that keep atoms together, like the electrons that circle around the center of an atom. Strong forces are the forces of energy it takes to pull apart an atom, like a nuclear explosion. That's it. That's all there is. Everything is made of one or more of these four kinds of energy. They have also determined that energy cannot be created from nothing, and energy cannot be destroyed into nothing. Energy can only be transformed into different states or be expressed at different wavelengths. Do you remember your old, outdated Newtonian physics from high school when they taught you that matter cannot be created or destroyed? I told you most of the good stuff I learned in high school… That basic law of Newton was almost right. But matter is made up of mostly energy and space. It is the energy and space that make up matter that cannot be created or destroyed. Remember that it's a fact that you are made up of mostly energy and space, so think about that for a second. Humans are just a coordination of specific information that exists as energy and space. Just like everything else that exists in the universe. This is one of those undeniable scientific facts that no one can argue, so it is worth remembering.

I hope I did not confuse or bore anyone too much with the information here. This is not just an interesting topic that you may want to explore at some time in the future, but it is related to the healing process, which takes "time," and very much related to the aging phenomenon. It does have a relation to what we are talking about here when it comes to health. I would refer you to any good book on quantum physics/quantum theory, and books written by Deepak Chopra, M.D., if you would like to investigate this further. For now just keep this concept in your mind as we continue.

So back to time...

Since time is a man-made concept, and it is thought about in a linear way by most, it has some inherent flaws in some of its man-given properties or concepts. Therefore many of the other "concepts" that we have that are related to or based on time, like aging, may also have some flaws. Most things we relate to time are negative, making time a negative thing in our lives. Terms like "Not enough time," "Wasting time," "Not enough hours in the day," and worst of all, "I'm running out of time," which means you're ready to die because "Your time is over," or "Time has run out," "Your time is up"! I strongly believe that focusing on anything that is negative is detrimental to your health, and in fact I will soon show you scientific facts and proof to support that in the chapter on stress. For now, I would like to get you to start thinking of your health totally removed from anything related to time, and in fact, totally removed from anything related to negativity. You do not have to get sick when you get older and that's a fact. Here are some interesting facts and studies that will help you solidify this concept:

Significant studies have been done on many cultures where the people live on an average to be over 100 years old. Many of the studies on the Georgian people of Russia show them to be vibrant at the age of 100, and many live to be 115 to 120 or more. Studies on the Indian tribal people of Mexico called Tarahumara Indians in the Sierra Madres Mountains show the same thing. In fact, in their culture one of the things they are known for is long-distance running. They believe that as you get older and wiser you also get better physically too. They believe it so strongly that it actually happens. The 40-year-old runners run faster and longer that the 20-year-old runners there. But that's nothing compared to the 60-year-old runners, who do even better. Similar tribes of very old people show the same thing in areas of Afghanistan, and the Hindu Kush Mountains of India. Studies from all over the world reveal these facts. Many experts have done studies for many years on each of these cultures, trying to find the secret to a long life. What do they all have in common? Until recently no one could find a common link. It was not in their diet. It was not their climate or weather. What was it?

Finally a study was done by Alexander Leaf, M.D., a doctor and professor from Massachusetts University, and also from Harvard Medical

School. He decided to get a list of biomarkers of aging together, and personally investigate all of these cultures of people who lived long and healthy lives. He actually spent time living among each culture. Surely there must be a common link. After many years of research and study he could not find a single common indicator of health and longevity except one. The only factor he ever found was the common *collective belief system* of the society. It was the collective consciousness of the culture that believed that you should get better as you get older, that made it happen. It was expected. "Expectation influences outcome" was his main conclusion from his years of study. It's the self-fulfilling prophecy. We all know this happens to individuals in society. We see it every day in our educational system. If a teacher thinks a student is smart and expects him or her to do well and also likes the student, that student will get an easy "A" in that class. A similar student that the teacher does not like, or that the teacher thinks won't do well, will struggle in that class and have no chance to get an "A." But when the same two students reverse roles with another teacher, their grades are opposite too! Self-fulfilling prophecy. Doctor Alexander Leaf won awards for his work, but nothing in medicine has changed because of it, even though many others have confirmed the findings of his research.

Another interesting bit of research, one that Deepak Chopra and other scientific researchers like to quote, is a study done by Ellen Langer in the mid 1980s. Ellen Langer is a psychologist and professor at Harvard Medical School. She wrote a great book called *Mindfulness*. Doctor Langer conducted what she called an experiment in time. She advertised in the *Boston Globe* newspaper for 100 elderly people to participate in a study. All 100 participants were over the age of 80. She then used a list of measurable biomarkers of aging to test each person. She had a list of almost 100 biomarkers of aging, including bone density, skin thickness, wrinkles, BMR, resting heart rate, vision, sugar tolerance, body temperature regulation, just about everything you would associate with changes of aging. She then took all the people to a monastery outside of Boston and told them to live exactly like they were in the 1950s. They were supplied with only 1950s stimulation. Elvis Presley music and other oldies, Alfred Hitchcock movies, Walter Cronkite news reports, restored 1950s cars parked outside, magazines and newspapers only from the 1950s, everything. They were told to "be" as you were in the 1950s. They even had name tags they had to wear all the time with pictures of them from the 1950s. A 1950s "environment" was created to the last detail. After only three weeks Dr. Langer measured the 100 biomarkers of aging again. In EVERY CASE their age was reversed by at least three years or more. Every biomarker of aging for every person showed him or her to be younger, physiologically! Even their wrinkles were reduced! How is that for solid evidence? 100% of the tests in 100% of the people, in only three weeks... imagine if they stayed for a year? Not bad, huh? But guess what? When they returned to Boston and weeks later they were tested again, all the biomarkers of aging reverted back again. More award-winning research. More confirmation by other researchers doing similar studies. Again no change in the practice of medicine at all.

Another interesting finding should be noted here about studies done on the native Alaskans. Most of them eat whale blubber; by the accounts of every clinical nutritionist in America, a very un-healthy diet. But they have fewer incidences of clogged arteries and heart disease than the general population of average Americans. Interestingly, when native Alaskans are transplanted to the Midwest and put on a low-fat vegetarian diet, they almost immediately develop diabetes, heart disease, and rotten teeth. Why? The native has been taken out of his environment that he was adapted to live in for thousands of years, for one thing, but also the stress of the new environment, along with the *expectation* of what will happen to his health by *observing the people around him*, combined to make real physiological changes in his mind as well as his body.

"Time goes you say? No, time stays, we go..."
Henry David Thoreau

To summarize all these interesting studies and state it in simple terms: Have you ever heard the expression "You get what you think about"? Well, that's pretty accurate. Your mind is a very powerful thing. The collective mindset of an entire population is even more powerful. Your mind, your thoughts, are directly influenced by those people who surround you. This is how an accepted trend starts. Why do you think every kid has to have a Cabbage Patch doll or a talking Elmo for Christmas? Why do you think teenagers have to have the latest pair of basketball sneakers? The only reason is because "society," whatever society they happen to be in, tells them they have to. It's just peer pressure and advertising. That exact same child, if transplanted to the South American jungle at a very young age, would not even think of owning any of those items, even if he saw them once on a television, if he ever saw a television. But I'm sure he would want to have the latest spear or knife. It is without a doubt that it's what the *collective consciousness of the society*, and what we as individuals "expect," that determines what our lives will be like. If we think like the crowd, we will be part of the crowd. Start getting sick when you're 50, retire when you're 60, move to Florida when you're 65, go to a nursing home when you're 70, die a horrible, disease-filled death when you're 80. That's what you're surrounded by, that is what society thinks is supposed to happen, so that is what you think is supposed to happen, and so it does.

Of course the typical American diet doesn't help. It is a known contributor to chronic degenerative disease. We'll fix that in a minute. But we must break the mold of how America thinks. I've just shown you a few of many studies that prove you can break the mold. There are hundreds more studies and real-life examples of people, individually and as a group, who have gone beyond what American society thinks "should" happen. Hundreds of examples of kids who "thought" themselves well from cancer, after chemotherapy and radiation had failed. Thousands of people who are now living to be 100 years old and beyond, not in a nursing home, but living happy and productive lives. So can you, and all of us, if we first change our mindset; we must change our ways of thinking. Nothing is more powerful than your mind. It is more your **thoughts** that create the world around you than anything else.

Your thoughts, emotions, opinions, and attitude *are* you. That's all that you are in fact. You are not your physical body. Remember, you are made up of energy and space. Energy and space cannot be created or destroyed, only changed. That is an undeniable fact that no one can argue. The study of quantum physics and the laws of thermodynamics prove it. The power to change your body and your life lies within your mind. You already have the power to do it. You need only think it, believe it, know it is true in your heart, soul, and mind, and in every cell of your body, and then just let the experience happen to you. Then use the other facts in this book to help support and maintain the new you that you have already crated in your mind. Healthy changes will become very easy.

It seems so simple that you may feel that it's just a far-fetched theory. But that's only because of all the memories of your past experiences that are telling you it might not be so. It's because of the words put into your head by your parents, your school teachers, your friends, your community. That's not reality; that's a created consciousness, based on the constant bombardment of misleading information from the misled people around you. That is the big lie. That is the "Hitler in Nazi Germany" that we discussed previously. Suppose that you heard nothing else all your life but the facts presented so far in this book. Suppose you were brought up in those Indian tribes, and raised to think that getting old is the greatest thing in the world. Suppose you lived in the Russian state of Georgia and were 114 years old, and riding your bike to go work in the fields. You would think that the accepted "American way of thinking" is absurd! Well, you would be right.

We were all once told that the world was flat. In fact, if you said differently the Church would have your head chopped off for blasphemy! Everyone strongly believed the earth was flat, or was killed for thinking otherwise. Now even the Church leaders will tell you the world is round. The same could be said for the earth being the center of the universe and the sun revolving around the earth. Yet no one accepts those big lies anymore either. But the resistance to these facts was great at the time.

Another truth about health is that perception, the power of your mind, is strongly related to health, and can actually determine your health status.

I hope the previous information has opened your mind a little bit. I think it's very important to keep an open and an objective attitude when we discuss certain topics that may seem new or different to you. If you would like more information on the things discussed so far, there are references listed in the back of the book. The topic of aging is very interesting and worth further investigation for most of you.

The things we will discuss from here on in are more concrete. Even though the following information may sound different from what you have previously learned, the facts and concepts should be easier to accept as true because they will be a little more "black and white" than the previous information. Plus now, hopefully, you have an open mind and will be a little more objective about the information and will not be so emotionally attached to your old ideas about health. Also I will be giving you real-life examples and solid scientific evidence in the text itself to support the information along the way, in addition to the list of references in the back of the book.

So let's answer some more "how's" and "why's," so when we come to the "do's" it will be easy. Since we all have a nervous system, and since I am a nervous-system doctor, I think this will be a good place to start. Let's learn "how" our bodies are made and how our function is influenced. It seems important to distinguish between that which is living and that which is not. I touched on this very briefly when we talked about humans being so much more than the sum total of all their parts. This question is essential to the study of living forms, yet a clear distinction continues to defy a concise scientific definition by most people. Many biologists continue to define life in very limited terms. They say life exists if the organism in question *"exhibits irritability to*

Dr. Bill F. Puglisi, D.C., C.C.W.P.

stimuli, responds to environmental change, has mobility, can metabolize food, can grow, and can reproduce"... etcetera...

Once again, right out of your old high school biology book, and confirmed by your college textbooks, word for word. But all "organisms" and all "nonliving things" are made of the same common building blocks. The atoms, molecules, and subatomic particles that are common to everything that exists are also united by the fact that they are all ultimately made up of the same exact thing, energy and space, as previously discussed. This is an accepted scientific fact. So how are these very similar array of particles organized in such a way as to work together to include, as part of their definition, *life*? How and when does it all happen? Well, there is little agreement on this point. Does life start at conception, or 24 weeks after conception, or in the third trimester, or at birth? This will not be a religious discussion but a logical, science-based discussion.

Think back in time... No, further back in time, to the time you were conceived, remember? What actually happened to animate conception itself? Is a sperm already life? Is an egg already life? What is the "force" or "energy" or "innate thought" that makes a sperm want to seek an egg and an egg to make chemical changes that allow for duplication of cells? Is life already "programmed" into eggs and sperm cells for generations before they ever get together, lying dormant until the right moment occurs for them to "think" about getting together for the purpose of procreation? These are the questions of life that religious leaders and great scientists ask everyday, yet can never seem to give a definite answer to. Both groups' conclusions depend upon faith, although much more faith is required for the strictly scientific points of view, since there are more and greater gaps in their explanation than in some religions explanations. A fact that many scientists themselves usually admit these days. Still there is no absolute proof, or at least agreement, of when "life" begins. To quote Gray's Anatomy 35th Edition from the chapter on embryology:

"To date, examinations of both the physical universe and the biosphere have led to fundamental generalizations concerning the nature of all forms of observation, and the interrelation of matter and energy. Aspects of energy are stated in various laws of thermodynamics, which hold that the total energy of the universe is constant, and that overall, the proportion of disorganized, randomized or dissipated energy[*1] (the entropy level) is steadily increasing. Living systems however, appear to reverse this trend by their growth, development, reproduction, and increasing structural complexity. That is to say, *their entropy level is* *decreasing.* This apparent paradox is only answered by considering life forms as *interlocked structurally, functionally, and energetically with their environment, from which they are supplied by a constant flow of energy which is essential for their maintenance."* (My emphasis)

This is the most widely accepted textbook used by every medical student in every medical school. Read it again and figure out exactly what it is saying. We are alive because some outside energy source supplies our body with energy. We are interlocked with our environment and are part of it, and can't be studied separately, but only together, since we are really the same thing.

It also goes on to say:

"Absolute dependency upon environmental energy emphasizes the dynamic nature of life processes whereby substances, *with the addition of energy**2, are transformed into complex molecules… any structural or functional organization is a complementary feature to its **environment**, and *they can only be studied together, that is, as one system**3." (My emphasis)

*1, *2, *3. **The world's leading scientific authority on the subject states above that life is energy. Life comes from energy, not parts. They also say that energy is constant, and cannot be created or destroyed (laws of thermodynamics). All things are made of similar energy and are related, and cannot be studied separately or as parts, but must be studied together, since they are part of the same environment. In fact, life exists totally dependent upon the environment that it is in, or more precisely, our energy that makes us alive is part of the energy of the universe, which is constant, not expanding or shrinking. Hopefully this will help you understand what I was saying earlier in this chapter about energy, and how everything is made of energy: the grain of sand, the mountain, and us. We are so closely interlocked that we cannot be separated, or even studied, separate from our environment. This is an important concept.**

There above lies indisputable scientific facts that basically blow up almost the entire practice of modern medicine. "We cannot be studied or treated as parts" We can only be studied and treated as a whole organism, and only in relation to the environment we are in.

A well-known Ayurvedic sage once said something to the effect of:

"You are the moon and the stars, you are the flower, and they are you."

Many similar quotes can be found in the study of Zen Buddhism and other philosophical and religious sources, (as well as many scientific sources). This is a more accurate statement than you think, and, in fact, very similar to many statements made by almost every major religion, philosopher, and scientist in all of history. These are the laws of thermodynamics. Yes, they *agree* with the scientists:

"Look within, thou art the Buddha..."
Buddha

"The Kingdom of heaven is within you..."
Jesus

And on and on... I could fill the page with similar quotes from both scientific and religious texts, but I think you get the point. The truth was always the truth. Almost everyone agrees on the truth, they just don't know it yet. They are saying the same things really; you are a glob of information, expressed mostly as energy and space, and you are part of the bigger glob of information, that is, identical to the energy and space that makes up the universe. They all just say this exact same thing differently, depending upon how scientific or religious they want to sound when they say it. And of course depending on their language, their culture, their scientific beliefs, their religious beliefs, and what their parents told them to say. For our purpose here, just remember that you are more than just the sum of your parts, you always were more than just the sum of your parts, and you will always be more than just the sum of your parts. It's that simple. Let them worry about what that "more" really is for now.

Let's get back to how we all got started.

Once the sperm does fertilize the egg (your opinion on how that really happens and what it means is fine; it doesn't really matter) the egg goes through a process called cleavage, in which all the inner material is divided in half, and then the entire cell divides into two identical cells. The resulting cells are called blastomeres, and each cell or blastomere continues to divide equally; 2 become 4, then 8, then 16, then 32, then 64, then 128... every 20 minutes or so. The growth rate is incredible. A thousand becomes 2000, then in only 20 minutes 4000, in 20 minutes 8000, then 16000, then 32,000 then 64,000. Soon there are literally millions. Two million become 4 million in 20 minutes, then 8 million, then 16 million, then 32 million, then 64 million. This continues for at least 19 days up to five weeks, with all the cells exactly identical, and none of them resembling any adult human cell, like a kidney cell or liver cell, or muscle cell. Then at about three to five weeks something happens called *"Gastrulation,"* where the cells start to become different. This is also called *"cell differentiation."* There are lots of fancy names for the cells becoming different, because once again, no one can really explain *why* the cells become different. The best geneticists and embryologists will talk circles around you trying to explain it, but no one really knows exactly what happens to make them become different; they only know when and how, but not why. This is one of the true mysteries of life. Call it; soul, spirit, The Great Spirit, Creator, Life, life-force, life energy, God, mind, chi, Manitou, Thetan, Mother Nature, innate, innate intelligence, cosmic power, or "Mighty Joe the Wonder Puppy"... you'll be just as accurate as they are. There is a whole section in *Gray's Anatomy* textbook titled "*The Modern View of Differentiation.*" It talks about eukaryotic cells and prokaryotic cells and "special interactions" and huge leaps of faith in one mans unproven evolutionary concepts, and is very interesting and purely conjecture, and a huge "leap of faith" in general, like Albert Einstein talked about. It's also in their embryology section if you care to go read it.

> *"You who are called by a thousand names, Mother Nature, may we all remember we are cells in your body and all dance together."*
>
> *Starhawk*

At this point, when cells become "different," three separate layers form, and the first definitive cells to form are those that make up the brain, spinal cord, and the nervous system. At this time cell death is occurring already, cell growth and continued differentiation is occurring, and waste removal is taking place. This can happen as early as 19 days! The instant that Mother Nature or "Mighty Joe the Wonder Puppy," or whoever, says "be different," it is difficult to argue that "life" has not begun! Of course people still do argue this point, even though the process described above is revealed in just about every anatomy book, every genetics book, and every embryology book that you could ever read. Oh well, not really pertinent to our discussion right now, but it may be later on, so keep it on the back burners.

The main point is that the first thing to develop in a human is the brain and nervous system, and it happens between 19 days and five weeks after fertilization. At this point most scientists refer to the developing human as an embryo, a term you are probably familiar with. Growth, development, and differentiation continue at a rapid pace, but for us, the interesting thing is that many of the "parts" of a human being grow directly from the nervous-system layer of the embryo. Neural buds grow from the nervous-system layer and develop into all the organs that make up your digestive system. From this nervous system layer all of your skin develops. So from the inner-most parts to the outer-most parts, much of your body develops from, and maintains direct contact with, your brain and nervous system. This should help you understand how your brain and nervous system controls everything in your body. A fact we will need to know and remember later on when we discuss getting healthy.

In this little anatomy lesson, please don't lose sight of the fact that you are not only your body. In fact very little of you is actually your body. You are mostly energy and space. Your body is the tool that you, as energy and space (soul, spirit, information, whatever) uses to express a level of physical existence. Your nervous system is the liaison, or the go-between, from you to your body and its parts. Your nervous system detects stimulus from the environment, and then sends signals to your body parts to react appropriately to the environment and help all parts work together as a team to maintain *"homeostasis,"* or balance. This happens for the single purpose of allowing your body to function in a healthy state. "Homeo" means self. "Stasis" means static or the same. This is an important word for you to know. The definition of health is maintaining *homeostasis*, or a constant balance of healthy function. The key point being that health is something that you, and your brain and nervous system, want your body to have. Health is normal. Health is natural. You and your brain and nervous system work very hard 24 hours a day to maintain health or homeostasis. Sickness and disease are unnatural undesirable states. They are not supposed to happen when you get older. They are not supposed to happen at all, EVER! You can prevent almost every chronic degenerative disease that you can think of. This is one of those undeniable facts that you should know. In fact I would all but memorize these last two paragraphs before continuing your reading. This is something that a lot of medical doctors don't want you to know. It's one of their big secrets.

Another truth about health is that health is mainly just <u>maintaining homeostasis</u>, which is the normal desirable state that your body wants to have at all times.

Homeostasis is health. Health is homeostasis. Think of a thermostat in your home. Its purpose is to maintain homeostasis in your environment with regard to temperature. You set the thermostat to 68 degrees, and the room temperature stays at 68 degrees. But is the mechanism or process that keeps the temperature static at that same 68 degrees, also static? No, the furnace is ever-changing. A fire ignites and burns. Energy is used. A fan blows the hot air to the rooms of the house, or a pump starts and pushes hot water through pipes in your radiators. The switch in your thermostat is constantly turning on and off. It is a system that is in constant motion to maintain homeostasis. This is how all the functions in your body work. The electrical wiring in the walls of your house is the connection and relay system, the nervous system, to and from the thermostat to the furnace, with branches going to the fan, and branches going to the water pump. Think of your body this way, except that your nervous system is processing about 300,000 bits of information from about 50,000 "thermostats" in your body and in your environment, every second of every minute of every day. Not only is this an impressive feat all on its own, but this all develops and is fully functional in about 37 weeks from the time of conception.

I like that word "conception" because it comes from the word "conceive," which means to realize or think about, or to start. Maybe your life starts as a "thought," an idea that the sperm and egg each have together, when they are placed in the same "environment." Remember, *environment* is really what determines everything. In a different environment that sperm and egg would not have the idea of getting together. Only being exposed to the proper environment gets them to react or think that way. Remember the scientific definition from *Gray's Anatomy* that said life is present if an organism responds to a stimulus, or reacts to its environment, and adapts… which is exactly what happens when a sperm and egg get together in the same environment. When they get together they immediately fit the definition of "life" as science states it and accepts it. So why the big argument on when life begins?

More on this later…

For now, just remember that your nervous system controls everything in your body. The main job is to maintain homeostasis or balance, so your body can remain healthy in its environment. Remember too that health is the normal, desirable state of existence that every cell in your body works on constantly to achieve and keep, for life. You are not supposed to get sick, ever!

> *"To take in a new idea you must destroy the old, let go of old opinions, to observe and conceive new thoughts. To learn is but to change your opinion."*
>
> B. J. Palmer

Chapter 4

Genetics 101
(More How's)

"It is not the answer that enlightens, but the question."
Eugene Ionesco

What about the genes? Don't they determine everything?

The short answer is no, genes don't really determine anything, at least not when it comes to most peoples' health. <u>We are about to bust one of the biggest myths in the current practice of medicine</u>. The paradigm of medicine is changing again, as it does every 100 to 200 years or so. Since the germ theory was busted and backfired on them, they need a new premise to base their treatment on, so they are all jumping on the gene bandwagon.

See, the medical profession must make a huge paradigm shift, or leap of faith, each time their paradigm, their dogma, their basis for "state of the art medical practice" gets exposed as unscientific.

In the beginning there was the witch doctor, voodoo doctor or "medicine man"; he would dance, and sing, and chant, and give out fresh herbs to treat the infirm of the tribe. Actually this was not a bad system for the time. It worked on many people.

Then it was discovered that more sickness and disease occurred when people lived near the swamps and watering holes, especially when these sources of water started to smell foul (from their own pollution of the swamp by their bathing, cleaning, swimming, and disposal of garbage and raw sewage, but they didn't know about hygiene yet). So the "Bad Vapor Theory" was the new paradigm shift. Medical experts decided to burn the swamp lands, which seemed to reduce the incidence of disease. This was state-of-the-art medical treatment for over a hundred years.

Then, when the Church came into great power and basically ruled the known "modern" world, it was thought that it was possession by "bad spirits" that caused most illness. The paradigm shifted again. Drilling holes in the heads of the infirm now became the state-of-the-art medical treatment of the time. This treatment, however, often resulted in death (go figure) and people started to reject this treatment.

Then someone discovered that blood circulated through the body, and when blood stopped circulating through the body, people died. So it must be bad blood that was the problem, and the "Bad Blood Theory" came into vogue. Bloodletting and leeches were the new state-of-the-art medical treatment. In fact, President George Washington was killed by this treatment, by the greatest and most respected medical doctors of his time.

Then, a hundred years later, after Anton Von Leeuwenhoek invented the microscope, bacteria were discovered. A new paradigm shift was necessary, and the "Germ Theory of Disease" was born. Surely it was bacteria that were the enemy, so we began the war against germs. Some doctors still try to push this disproved paradigm on you once in a while, even though most of "modern" medicine has abandoned it. The problem was that germs were always there and always will be there, with every breath we take, and every object we touch, but most people are not dying of infection, or even getting sick. Thousands of different bacteria and viruses are commonly found on, and in, the healthiest of people, the *exact same* bacteria and viruses found on and in sick people. It was not the germ that was the problem, it was the "host," the weakened body that sometimes allowed the germ to multiply and take over. Time to change our minds again....

What about them genes? They determine everything, sort of, don't they? Sickness must be "programmed" into us. The present paradigm shift is now towards genetics.

Back to high school biology again:

Back in John F. Kennedy High School I had a great biology teacher named Mrs. Petrone. We did lots of cool experiments with bacteria (and never got sick). We made slides and looked at chromosomes under the microscope. And we learned about genes. Genes are merely the "blueprints" of how to make stuff that our bodies need. Genes are the "directions" for baking the cake; for making the cells and cell parts, and chemicals in our bodies. Remember, they are the little amino acid structures, the building blocks of proteins, that lay dormant in the nucleus of every cell in your body, until called upon by the signals of the body to reproduce some cell part or chemical as needed to function normally. Genes do not have a mind of their own. They do not tell the body what to do, or what to make. The signal that the cell sends to the nucleus tells the protein of the DNA structure, the protector and holder of the genes, what genes to "express" based on environmental needs. The only misconception that is often taken from the study of genetics is that the nucleus is the brain of the cell. It is not. Genes are just the files in the file cabinet of our cells, not the brains. In fact, most of the best cellular biologists on earth will now tell you that it is the cell membrane that is the real brain of the cell. It is the cell membrane that determines what signal or "message" will be sent to the DNA to activate a gene sequence. It is the cell membrane that senses the environment and reacts to the environment first. The cell membrane controls what signal is sent to the particular gene sequences.

If you take a nucleus out of a cell and study it in the lab, it can be kept viable for a long period of time if conditions are right. But if you take a cell membrane and try to do anything at all to it, it dies immediately. If you open up your high school biology book (or college text, or most advanced books on genetics; they are all the same), you will see that all the gene sequences, the amino acids lined up in different orders, are wrapped up in the double helix structure of the DNA, which is covered by many different protein molecules. In order for a gene to be exposed or expressed, the protein cover must be "unlocked." To unlock the protein cover, the DNA is sent a message (messenger RNA) that is controlled by the signal that the cell membrane gets from its environment. Are you paying attention? Write this down: IT IS THE SIGNALS THAT THE CELLS GET FROM THEIR ENVIRONMENT THAT DETERMINE WHICH GENES ARE EXPRESSED! This is one of those undeniable facts of life that no one can deny. It is simple biology. Ask Dr. Bruce Lipton M.D., Ph.D., or any other world's leading authority on genetics, or cellular biology. The cell must get a "signal," a stimulus from the environment, which is interpreted by the cell membrane, and then sent to the DNA by a messenger, to tell the DNA to expose a sequence of genes to reproduce what the cell thinks it needs to maintain homeostasis and health, *according to what is happening in its environment.*

Genes do not change within an organism. It takes generations for mutations to take place, because when the perfect blueprint is tampered with by a mutation, the rest of the cell destroys it. If you are born with normal healthy genes, then you have the same normal healthy genes when you're 5 days old, 5 weeks old, 5 months old, 5 years old, and 55 years old! AND, these normal healthy genes make normal healthy cells, cell parts, and chemicals. They can't do anything else. They don't know how to do anything else. They are only the blueprints. They are only amino acids, lined up in a certain order or sequence that never changes. The human gene pool has not changed significantly in almost 50,000 years! Every day you can read in the news or see on TV that a new gene sequence has been "discovered" that can cause a certain health problem. The fact is that sicknesses from gene "defects" are responsible for less than 1% of all sickness and disease on earth. You can quote me on that. Or you can quote all the leading medical experts on the planet who say so. Just go look it up. Go ahead, I'll wait…

See, I told you. It's well documented. And those genetic "diseases" also have not changed in the past 50,000 years either. So what about the newly "discovered" genes for obesity? What about the gene that was just discovered for alcoholism? What about the "hangover gene" that was just in the newspaper in 2006? So what! Any improper gene sequence can be unlocked by the messenger proteins and get expressed if the interpretation of the environment is one of stress or abnormality. Remember the body wants to be healthy and maintain homeostasis or balance. If the environment changes, then the body has to adapt its physiology in order to survive in the new environment. But remember it is the bad signal from the bad environment that is the problem, NOT the gene itself. Sure, some people have the bad gene sequence and some do not. But the contractor is asking for the wrong set of blueprints. Did the people with the hangover gene have a hangover every single day since the day they were born? For example, let me ask you this simple question and see if you can answer it for yourself. Let's say we all had the gene for obesity. If we all ate only healthy food, and exercised properly every day, and burned up more calories than we took in, could we be obese? Let's say we all had the alcoholism gene, and we all had the hangover gene. If we never drank alcohol could we get drunk? If we did not drink alcohol yesterday, could we have a hangover today? I'll give you a hint: NO!

See, it's not the *gene* that "*causes*" the hangover, it's the *alcohol!* It's the *environment* of the cells. No matter what genes you have, as long as they were normally expressing health when you were 5 years old, then they will express health when you are 55 years old, and 105 years old. They have no choice. Only the stressful environment can make the cells of your body send improper messages to the DNA to get the wrong "unhealthy" gene sequence to be expressed, or cause the gene sequence to change in some way. I will put my professional license on the line right now, and ***promise*** you that no matter what genes you have, if you do not drink any alcohol, you will not get drunk, and you will not have a hangover! If any medical experts wish to argue that point, please give them my number and have them contact me.

I wonder what paradigm shift will take place next so that the medical establishment will have something to hang their hats on, to continue to push drugs and surgery. Personally, I hope they go back to the original

Witch Doctor, since they did as much good and certainly less harm, than some current medical practices.

Anyway, the whole point of this chapter is to get you to realize that you don't have to be sick because your genes are "programmed" for sickness. They are not. Genes are programmed for health. Genes have not changed much over the past years, and it is almost impossible for them to change from healthy genes to sick genes within one person's lifetime. If you were born with a genetic defect, then that won't change either, and that gene will be expressed. But if you were born with normal healthy genes, like more than 99% of the world population, then those genes will not change either. If you were expressing healthy genes at 5 days old and at 5 years old, then you can and should express only healthy genes all the time at any age. It is only when you create an unhealthy environment for your body's cells, one that causes some kind of toxicity, or some kind of deficiency of required healthy ingredients, that gene expression can be affected. This is because your body's physiology must "adapt" to the new condition of the environment in order to change cellular function for survival. Genes are programmed to function normally in a healthy environment, with healthy food, healthy exercise, healthy air, and healthy water as the required raw ingredients to allow the body to maintain homeostasis.

The truth about health is that health does not come from your genes; health comes from sufficiency and purity of your environment.

Your genes are not able to make what is required to help your body digest the heavy-metal toxic poisons that are put into the fertilizer used to grow your food on most conventional American farms, for example. They are not programmed to deal with the abnormally high amounts of chlorine, lead, arsenic, and fluoride in your drinking water that was not there 50, 40, 30, 20, and 10 thousand years ago. We have changed the environment. We have altered what goes into our body and are forcing the cells to adapt to a toxic environment that they cannot handle. The cell membranes are getting a signal of stress in the environment and are sending a message to the DNA to express gene sequences that don't really exist to handle that particular stress. Here lies the real problem. This is the real basis of almost all illness and disease. The response to a stress in the environment results in an "adaptive," or "abnormal," physiology that is signaled by some type of toxicity, or the deficiency of a required healthy ingredient needed to maintain homeostasis. That's it.

More than 99% of all illness and disease can be traced to some toxicity or some deficiency of a required ingredient for health.

Everything I had to know about genes I learned from Mrs. Petrone in high school biology class; I just didn't know it yet. When I went to college I took courses in genetics, nutrition, and in microbiology. Those long and expensive courses taught me the same thing. When I went to professional graduate school I took more courses covering genetics, microbiology, cell physiology, nutrition, and biochemistry. They also taught me the same thing. After graduating and becoming a doctor, I took continuing education courses in nutrition, and in technical courses that covered genetics and cellular biology, that taught me the same thing. Just like the gene pool of humans, this basic, truthful information did not change from year to year or from course to course. I guess right is right. I guess truth is truth. Please try to understand this basic principle very well before continuing, because it will be coming up again a few times before we are done. More proof to support the facts stated here about genes will be coming too, so don't worry. Just remember... "It's not the *gene*, it's the *stress signal*!" (Have I said that enough times yet?)

Chapter 5

Stress Or *Distress*

"We can easily forgive a child who is afraid of the dark; the real tragedy of life is when adults are afraid of the light."

Plato

Let's review:

I'm from Paterson, New Jersey.

I didn't find most of college time useful.

Most of what I know I learned growing up at the lake or in high school, or on my own, anyway.

Human beings are more than just the sum of their parts.

I should have died when I was a kid but a Chiropractor saved my life when M.D.'s couldn't.

I don't like drug companies.

I do like getting to the basic truth of the matter.

You can make changes in your life and be healthy, but only if you really want to.

Your mind/attitude is the most powerful thing you have to improve your health and your life.

Times sure have changed since I was a kid, but genes haven't.

It's not about the gene; it's about the signal from the environment.

That pretty much covers it.

We're almost half way there, only five chapters to go after this…

This chapter on stress may by the most important information in this book for some of you. So we need to define stress, and also differentiate that from "distress." We will also have to learn what distress, or the "stress response" does to your body to make you unhealthy. Then we can figure out ways to slow down, stop, and even reverse this negative response of your body, and get you truly healthy again. It sounds easy, but there's a lot more to it. That's ok, don't stress…

It's not *just* that the environment has changed that's causing stress on and in your body. It is actually the way you interpret the stress, and how you react to it, that is what really matters the most. Remember what we said about how your mind is a very powerful thing, and that your general attitude is very important, as it relates to your health? Well that will be key to our discussion here.

The classic definition of stress won't really help you much, but here it is...

Stress means " to strain, to have pressure, to have emphasis. It also means a special force on an object, a person, or a part of speech."

Not a lot of help, I know. For example, where does this "force" or "pressure" come from? It mostly comes from you. Your perception is a key factor to the kind of stress that we are talking about here. Now of course there are some outside forces that cause stress on our bodies, like gravity for instance, that we can't control. But this is constant and we have adapted to it over the past 50 thousand years or so. There is also air pollution that may be creating a stress response in your body, because you are not programmed to handle that particular toxin that you may be inhaling, as we have previously mentioned. Also keep in mind, that some stress is good, like exercise. Exercise "stresses" your muscles, tendons and joints. But when controlled and done properly, this is actually beneficial. So some stress can be good for you especially, if you "think" it is good for you and really believe it. Exercise is natural and is a required ingredient for health. Our genes are programmed for exercise, and again we have adapted to it over the past 50 thousand years, because it was a necessary part of daily life for that long. Now in the industrialized modern society that we live in, exercise has become a minimal part of our life, and this lack of exercise has become more stressful to our bodies than the stress of exercise itself; does that make sense?

Don't worry, it gets easier. Plus there will be a whole chapter on exercise where we will explore this further. Let's get to the "bad" stress that we can control. The stress that causes bad things, the kind that causes "adaptive physiology" to occur in your body.

We will be learning three basic sources of stress that affect your body in a negative way; physical stress, chemical stress, and mental or emotional stress. Most people are familiar with the mental stress. That is what most people commonly think of when they hear the word "stress." This is the "my job is giving me an ulcer" kind of stress. But to illustrate the point that it's how stress is "interpreted" that is also important, let me relate this story:

It is a beautiful spring morning. The temperature is perfect and your bedroom window is half open. Outside in the backyard tree, a beautiful songbird wakes you up to the sweet sound of nature's music. You sit on the edge of your bed and smile. You go to the window to open it further, to get the full sound and full view of Mother Nature's wonder. You stretch and yawn and think to yourself, "What a perfect way to wake up in the morning... life is good!"

Across from your yard is your neighbor's house. He wakes up on this same fine spring day to the sound of the same bird, singing the same song, in the same tree. He sits on the edge of his bed, but does not smile. He looks out the half-opened window and curses the bird for waking him up. He gets up screaming and cursing and slams the window shut!

The question is: Where is the source of the stress? Is it the bird singing? See, the same environmental stimulus can cause very different physiological responses in each human being. Some would be calm and happy, some would be frustrated and angry, and for another there may be total indifference, not even noticing the bird at all, or just not letting the bird affect them physically. And make no mistake about it, there *is a physical response* happening in the body of each of those individuals in the story above. That response is what this chapter is all about.

Just substitute *"the singing bird"* for any external stimulus, like "that comment my spouse made," or "that thing that happened at work yesterday," or "that news report I heard tonight." Any of these can cause the same negative "stress response" or adaptive physiology in your body, or not, depending upon how you allow it to affect you, or how you "interpret" the stimulus.

Over thousands and thousands of years, the human body has adapted a special physiological response to negative stimuli. It is called the "stress response" or, back to our high school biology class again, the "fight or flight" response. It works like this:

Your nervous system detects a stimulus, like hearing the singing bird. Your nervous system has many specialized ways of detecting stress, like seeing, hearing, smelling, tasting, and touching or feeling, which can be further broken down into feelings of pressure, pain, heat, cold, tingling, and vibration. Once your nervous system detects a stimulus, it usually has to send a message to your spinal cord or brain to get that stimulus "interpreted" so the proper response can be elicited by your body. Your brain or spinal cord interprets the stimulus as "good," "bad," or "indifferent," meaning no significant physiological response is necessary. If it is a "good" stimulus, like a bird singing in the morning, this positive stimulus is called "proprioception" by most neurologists, and a "proprioceptive response" is started by your nervous system. This could include promoting a healthy blood pressure, a slower heart rate, a lower blood sugar level, and even lower cholesterol levels in your blood. However, if the stimulus is "bad" (threatening or negative in some way), like that darn bird singing in the morning, this negative stimulus is called "nociception," and a nociceptive response is started by your nervous system. This can include raising your blood pressure, speeding up your heart rate, causing your blood sugar to rise, and even raising your cholesterol. These terms come from studying pain and pleasure differences in the nervous system, and have to do with nerve pathways for touch and for "feeling" in general, but the same pathways (nerve fibers) are used for almost all positive and all negative stimuli that will result in this response. Don't worry about the big fancy medical words. Just get the concept. Now here is the interesting fact. ALL the cells in your body, all 50 trillion or so, can have this response, and not only that, all 50 trillion cells can have this response at the exact same time! WOW!

This is amazing but true. This fight or flight response was necessary thousands of years ago when man was confronted with a threatening or "stressful" situation; for example, being chased by a tiger in the jungle. Back then even the nociceptive response or the "bad" response was good in a way, at least for a short time. This response prepares your body to fight or run, both of which would require these physiological changes. It is a survival response. It is a normal response. For example it is good to have extra sugar in your blood when running or fighting to use as energy. It is good to have your heart rate go faster to pump blood to your muscles that you will be using. It is good to have the digestion process slow down, another one of many things that changes from this response, and instead use that energy to fight or run. Digestion is not that important when you're about to be eaten by a tiger... well, maybe it is for him, but not for you.

So this is a normal response, but it's supposed to happen only for a short time. When you are safe from the tiger, the physiology changes back to normal again. It is very important to keep in mind that when this happens, when your body cells change their physiology, that you are not really "sick." Remember, if you have healthy genes making healthy body parts, then that does not change. The actual function of the cell changes to "different" physiology, that's all. The neurological and hormonal pathways that are involved in this process are a little complicated, but I think worth mentioning briefly. First, here's what happens:

1. Your nervous system detects a stimulus as an abnormal situation in the environment (stress) and responds APPROPRIATELY, with the fight or flight response.

2. Your sympathetic nervous system sends signals to your brain and other organs, to change their function (on a cellular level).

3. The adrenal glands produce adrenaline. This hormone causes increased blood pressure, increased heart rate, and increased respiration. You're getting ready to run or fight.

4. Signals are sent to the adrenal cortex to produce Cortisol. This hormone causes decreased insulin, another hormone. (Which results in increased blood sugar)

5. The general immune response of your body decreases, and growth hormone decreases. (It is not that useful to fight infection or work on growing, when you're being eaten by a tiger.) This can also causes fatigue and sleepiness due to constant stimulation if prolonged for a while.

6. Fatty acids and fat-based hormones in the blood are increased, including cholesterol.

7. Cognitive brain function decreases, and it becomes hard to concentrate (no use in doing algebra when your leg is being chewed off).

8. A whole host of other things too numerous to mention occur, all preparing you to run or fight.

This is the fight or flight response. This is the stress response. It is also called the hypothalamic-pituitary-adrenal axis response, because these are the main neurological and hormonal pathways involved. I mention them for the doctors that may be reading this book. Please get out your old physiology and neurology textbooks and study these pathways. Or just read Doctor James Chestnut's first book. As a treating doctor you must know this response, how it works, and why it happens this way. For the general reader (and for the doctor), know this key fact: *this is a normal response*. It is supposed to happen and does happen *all the time, every time* in the presence of stress. It is reversed when the stressor is removed. When you are safe from the tiger, everything goes back to normal. If the stressor is not removed, this physiological reaction remains indefinitely. (EVERYONE memorize this important paragraph).

Think of another example. If I sneak up behind you and scare you, how long does it take for your heart to pound, your hair to stand on end, and your palms to get sweaty? It happens in a fraction of a second. When you turn around and see it is only me, immediately the process is reversed, but it takes a little longer to get back to normal. Once the hormones are released into the blood stream it takes a while, a few minutes to a few hours, for things to "calm down" again after the stress is removed. But remember you were not sick. Your cells just temporarily changed their physiology.

The question you have to ask now is, "What if the stressor is not removed?" This is the million dollar question that so few doctors seem to ask. Remember the three main stressors I mentioned earlier, physical, chemical, and mental stress? Well as it turns out, it does not matter what the stressor is, the stress response is the *same*, all the time every time! So what are physical stressors? Bumps and bruises from slips and falls, "subluxation" of your joints, and other joint problems like arthritis, broken bones, cuts, and tiger bites... it doesn't matter because they all cause the same response, the stress response. What about the chemical stressors? These are air pollution, tap water, junk food, smoking, drinking alcohol, taking drugs, pesticides on foods, using microwave ovens, using Teflon pans, using most household cleaners, using most commercial make-up products, hair dyes, anti-perspirant, etc… it does not matter because they all cause the same response, the stress response. What are the emotional stressors? Things like anger, aggression, hate, worry, money problems, job problems, family problems, spouse problems, fear, anxiety, etc... it doesn't matter because they all cause the same response, the stress response. This is one of those undeniable scientific facts, so please make sure you get this point. It does not matter if the stress is a physical, chemical, or emotional/mental stress; it is causing the stress response, all the time every time, at some level!

Every one of the things mentioned on the list of eight reactions above, and a whole lot more, is what happens with any stressor that is interpreted by your nervous system as negative, (or nociception).

Now let's suppose that you have an undetected subluxation in your spine that is not causing you pain, but it is affecting your joint or nerve in a negative way. And let's suppose you are worried about paying off your college loans. And let's suppose you just ate lunch at McDonalds. Your system is stressed! But you don't "feel it" in a very conscious way. And let's suppose that you decide to go to a doctor for a check-up because things don't seem right, even though you feel "o.k." You wait for an hour in the doctor's office. More stress. You're afraid of the needle used to take the blood test. More stress. The nurse hurt you when she sticks the needle in your arm. More stress. She draws blood and sends it out to be tested. What do you think the results will be? Review the eight things above related to the stress response. High blood sugar, high blood cholesterol, high blood pressure, etc... So what does the doctor say to you when you get the results? "You're sick!" But you are not sick. Remember again that you have normal healthy genes, making normal healthy cells and chemicals. But once the gene makes the cell, the cell gets the signal of stress from your nervous system and the cell changes its physiology in adaptation to the stress. If you remove the stress, the healthy cells will change their physiology back again to healthy physiology because they were not diseased cells. They were healthy all along. You were healthy all along. You were just responding appropriately to stress.

But the doctor who is treating your blood test, and make no mistake about it, the doctor is treating your blood test, not you... he will not ask the proper question, which is: WHY are these numbers so high? He will only ask the questions that he knows he has the answers to, like, "do I have something to give to you that will lower these numbers?" And of course he does; he has drugs that will lower your blood pressure, lower your blood sugar, and lower your cholesterol. You are now instructed to take these drugs and then go back to get another blood test so he can examine the two tests. Not so he can examine you because that would be too hard and take too much time, and he doesn't care about your student loans anyway. He only cares about the numbers on his blood test. Sure enough, when you go back, the numbers are down a little, and he is happy. He increases your dose of medicine and then later takes another blood test. Finally your blood test numbers are down; forced down artificially by the three toxic chemicals he gave you, the drugs, which are causing more stress to your body. But that's o.k., because when you die from ignoring the real cause, you die with low blood pressure, low blood sugar, and low cholesterol, so he is happy because his paperwork is neat and clean.

This is not an exaggeration. This is exactly what is happening to millions of people out there every day. There are almost 400,000 people dying every year just from "properly prescribed" drugs taken the "proper" way. This is a 9/11 terrorist attack happening every single day 365 days a year just in the United States alone, and no one is doing anything about it. Certainly not the drug companies or the FDA. Add to that the 600,000 other deaths from medical mistakes each year and that's about a million people being killed by the modern medical paradigm. And that is the reported statistics from the CDC, the W.H.O., and the insurance companies. Imagine all the medical mistakes that happen that don't get reported, or get reported as some other cause rather than a mistake? Do you think that might happen? The number is probably much greater than a million. Take into account that heart disease is considered the number one killer in America, with 940,000 deaths each year and rising. So what is the real number one killer in the United States? Obviously the practice of medicine, at least according to nutritionist and author Gary Null, and other experts. Actually you don't even have to be an expert; just look up these statistics from the CDC and W.H.O. and add them up. You don't need medical experience, just a calculator.

This could be why the United States is now ranked 37th on the World Health Index. We used to be number one in 1950, but have been declining steadily ever since. Less than 10 years ago we were ranked 21st. Even with all the advancing medical technology. Even though we have more doctors, nurses, hospitals, and more drugs than most of those other countries combined. How could this be? The United States is officially ranked 50th on the life expectancy scale. We used to be near the top of the list in 1950, but we have declined steadily ever since then. Even though we have the most technologically advanced medical system in the world. Even though with only **5%** of the world's population, the United States consumes **65%** of the world's drugs. Sadly, the United States has been ranked 74th on the quality of health care index. This means that you could go to 73 other countries in the world and get an all-around better quality of care based on case success rate and patient satisfaction, than you can get here. How can this be? We have the most doctors and the most hospitals. We have the most drugs and the most technology. I'm guessing that the reason we are ranked so low in these three categories is that we have the most doctors, and the most hospitals, and the most drugs and the most technology, so we use them! Even when it is usually overkill (a good word to use here) and we don't really need them. What we need is more common sense, education of the public, and some old fashioned caring and compassion. Banning prescription drug commercials from TV would be a great help too. Even many medical doctors hate the drug commercials. The M.D.s I've talked to say that patients come into their office asking for the drug they saw on a TV commercial, and if they don't get a prescription for it, they get upset. Some even go out to seek another doctor to get that prescription. If the medical doctor does not give them what they want, he stands to lose the patient, so some comply, even though it may not be in the patients' best interest to take that particular drug. They consider this a big problem because they actually care about the patient, but if they don't give the patient what he wants, they know that there is someone out there who will. Yes, there are a lot of great medical doctors out there who do care. Many of them are my friends and some are even my patients. Medical doctors who do the research are my biggest resource for the facts that am presenting in this book. I don't hate medical doctors; I hate drug companies as a big business and the stomach-turning alliances they have with the government and the AMA. They have too much power over the government, the medical doctors, the medical schools, and you. I agree with many M.D.s that is the real and significant problem affecting the health of the entire country.

Let's drive home the point about stress in your body. Remember that it is a normal response of healthy cells. If they did not respond this way you would not survive at all. The response can be reversed but only if you remove the stressor, not by adding drugs or other stressors. That will never work. Also remember that it does not matter if it is anxiety at work, the cheeseburger and fries, or the subluxation of your spine. They all cause the exact same stress response, all the time every time. They must be removed if you want to express optimum health. Some stressors cannot be removed very easily, like quitting the job you hate, or getting your college loans paid off by this Friday. This book is about the many stressors that you can remove easily. Removing any stress automatically increases your level of health. I will show you in future chapters how to deal with physical stress and chemical stress. You will be healthier when you try the changes that I recommend. But what about that mental/emotional stress? That's just as important but is a little tougher to reduce.

Here are some interesting facts about that kind of stress and some techniques that may help you in dealing with stress. A study done at the University of Washington Medical School tried to scientifically rate stressful situations both by survey and by the measurable negative physical effects on the health of the person. The death of a spouse was rated as the highest level of stress, having the most negative physical and mental/emotional effects. Divorce was the next most stressful circumstance, followed by marriage problems, and then *serious personal illness*. That's right, of the top four stressors, just being sick causes enough stress to make you even sicker. Once again as mentioned previously, fear and anxiety actually change cell function in your body, making you ill. Their study also concluded that the more stressful situations a person had, the greater their chance of getting any illness. Well, hopefully you already knew this by now. Dr Hans Selye, in his book *"Stress Without Distress,"* says that it is not the stress itself that is harmful; it is the *distress* that stress causes. Distress is what happens when stress is not dealt with in a positive way or in a timely manner. Remember the man being chased by a tiger? His system was stressed, but he remained healthy because he dealt with the stress the right way, he ran away to safety, or killed the tiger. He removed the stress so he was not distressed.

The most common signs of someone with prolonged stress are fatigue, headache, heartburn, indigestion, insomnia, and hair loss. The more serious conditions related to stress are backache, depression, hypertension, ulcers, impotence, and even cancer. Do you think mental stress and the conditions that it causes should be treated with toxic chemicals like drugs, or do you think it would be better to remove the stressor?

I like to tell people to deal with stress this way:

Get a pencil and blank sheet of paper. Go ahead and get them now, I'll wait...

Now draw two equal size empty cups or glasses. Each glass represents a person's load of stress. One of the cups is you, and the other one is your neighbor. Your neighbor is about the same age as you, the same sex, and even works for the same company where you work. Now mark the side of the cup with a notch or line for each stress in your life (See Picture #1 below). Start with family, but don't forget that your neighbor has some family stresses too, so you both have one line marked. Then consider work. But don't forget that your neighbor has similar work problems so they get a line too. Now you both have two lines. Consider your financial difficulties, but don't forget that you neighbor has a big mortgage and his credit cards are maxed out, so give him a notch on his cup also. Now you have three notches each. Now think about that horrible commute to work every day, but your neighbor has to deal with that too, so each of your cups gets another notch. Your cup of stress is getting full. Now let's think about the stress we mentioned before. You are not exercising properly or regularly, but you neighbor is, so only you get this mark on your cup of stress. You have not been eating well either. The bagels for breakfast and the fast-food lunches are catching up with you so you get another line on the side of you glass, but your neighbor has been brown-bagging it and says he is "into health food," so he does not get a notch for poor diet, only you. You know, you have not been sleeping too well lately; you toss and turn and get up in the middle of the night and you find yourself yawning after lunch. Another line for your cup of stress, but not your neighbor who seems to be sleeping better than you. You have also noticed a stiff neck occasionally when you get up in the morning, and you back hurts a little if you sit too long at work without moving. You may have a subluxation in your spine. Anyway, pain is not normal; it is a sign that something is wrong, so another notch for you. But your neighbor goes to a chiropractor, and he never complains of stiffness or back pain. No notch for his cup. Well, your cup of stress is almost full to the top.

(You can mark your cups right here in the book, using these pictures.)

Now you and your neighbor decide to carpool to work today. Unfortunately when you're sitting in that traffic, you get rear-ended, kind of hard, by another car. Your neck or back really hurts the next day, and so does your neighbor's, so he talks you into going in to see his doctor. After careful evaluation the doctor determines that you both have equally significant injuries, including subluxations, or misaligned spinal bones, both sustained in the same car accident.

You both treat these identical injuries the same way by the same doctor. Everything seems equal. But things were not equal. Your cup of stress has now overflowed. Your neighbor just got another notch, his cup was not full. So after six months your neighbor is 100% recovered, but after eight months you're still treating, and are only at about 80% better. Why? If you have the same injuries (physical stress) and the same treatment, then you should get the same results. Well, not always. Your cup of stress was too full. And after the accident you did not change your diet, your exercise program, or your sleep routine. You continued to try to deal with more stresses than your neighbor, and you will never fully recover until you make the changes necessary to reduce the stressors that are within your control. Your nervous system is overloaded, trying to deal with too many stressors at once.

(Mark your cup as overflowing.)

But now, after you have read this book, you decide to give it a try, and reduce all the stresses that are under your control. You change your diet. Erase one line off of your cup of stress. You also start the proper exercise program. Erase another line off of your cup of stress. You start to try some deep-breathing techniques, yoga, or other things to help you relax and you start to sleep much better. Erase another notch off of your cup. You decide to continue to go to a Subluxation-Based Wellness-Chiropractor who is specially trained in nutrition, exercise, and specific spinal correction. He takes an interest in your case and develops a customized plan for you to follow, based on the information found in this book. He does not give you general spinal manipulation, but instead very carefully and very specifically "adjusts" your spine, by hand, and explains to you how this will "correct" your spine. He then shows you very specific things to do at home to speed up and maintain this correction. You start to feel great. Better than you have ever felt before. You decide on your own to go to the chiropractor to get your spine checked and maintained once or twice a month, forever. You do this because it makes sense to you to prevent problems before they start. Not because you were told to. That would be stressful. You want to go because it makes sense, because it feels good, and most of all because the chiropractor showed you indisputable scientific research done by experts, many of them medical doctors, that proved to you that it makes sense without question, experts that not only recommend continued chiropractic care, but also go to the chiropractor themselves. They want to keep their cup of stress as low as possible, so the stress in their lives that they do have will be easier to deal with. You do it because you really want to and you see the results. Not because someone told you to do it. No one is forcing better health care on you; it's your choice, and you can stop whenever you want. Always stress-free.

I will cover more on the science of chiropractic care in the next chapter to prove all this, but let me give you one more little technique to deal with some of the stresses in your life.

One of the best things I have ever come across in my research on stress is the technique of writing down things that are important in you life. Make a list of all the priorities in life that are positive, worthy ideals and goals. This technique is taught by Anthony Robbins, who stole it from Wayne Dyer, who stole it from Dale Carnegie, who stole it from Earl Nightingale... and many other motivational speakers over our time. They charge you thousands of dollars to attend their weekend seminars and buy their tapes and CDs. They just change the words around, but they all say pretty much the same thing. So I'm going to steal from them and give you a little of it right here. One thing I will say for all these fine gentlemen, they steal really good stuff, and these things really do work if you do them exactly the way I describe them.

Simply get a pen and two sheets of paper, and make two lists. The first list should contain a short sentence on each of your goals and/or priorities in your life. Make sure these are positive and worthy (and achievable) goals that will benefit not only you but the people around you as well. The list should **not** include "I hope I win the lottery" or "I wish my neighbors barking dog would die." The first is not likely to be achievable, and the second is not that positive. Your list should include things like:

MY LIFE'S PRIORITIES AND GOALS

1. A close spiritual connection (to God, Creator, Nature, or to Mighty Joe the Wonder Pup, whatever...)
2. Better health
3. Improved personal relationships
4. Closer family ties

5. Better communication skills
6. Career goals, job promotion (or changing jobs)
7. Putting your child through college
8. A dream vacation for the family
9. Finish reading this book without falling asleep

Keep this list to 10 items or less. Keep adding to and subtracting from the list until you think you have got it right. Then, spend at least a few days on trying to prioritize this list. Put the most important things on top and the less important things at the bottom. This is hard to do and should take at least a few days or more. Each day you may feel differently about the priority of a goal, depending on what is going on in your life at the time. In fact, the order of this list may continue to change over time, depending on how close you are to some of these ideas, and other factors. So it won't be perfect. That's o.k. It won't be the same as everyone else's list. That's o.k. too. You can use the sample list above if you want. The only important thing is that you have a list written out.

Now take the second sheet of paper and pick an item from your list and write it down at the very top of the second piece of paper. This is going to be the goal that you want to achieve. Review your list and see what you want to improve by the end of the year and make it your number one goal. Let's take improved health for an example. That's a little general. We need some action steps to help us work toward that goal. So under the goal of improved health, or whatever you picked for your next achievable goal, we are going to make another short list. This one is easier than making the first list. It will only be four items numbered 1 through 4, like this:

<u>WORTHY GOAL...</u>

1. What will I do <u>today</u> that will help me achieve my goal...
2. What will I do <u>this week</u> to help me achieve my goal...
3. What will I do <u>this month</u> to help me achieve my goal...
4. What will I do <u>this year</u> to help me achieve my goal...

So far so good. You now have a "to-do" list. Now for the secret to success: DON'T DO ANYTHING ON YOUR LIST (yet). After you write this list you must read it out loud twice, everyday. Read it once in the morning when you first wake up. Then put it on your pillow and forget about it until you go to bed at night, then read it again. Reading this list out loud should only take you about 10 or 15 seconds. But the key is, even after you have it memorized, you must still take it out and read it out loud. You must use all your senses. You must touch it. You must see it, and you must hear it. But don't do anything else. Other than reading it out loud every morning and every night, forget about it. If you put pressure on yourself to do something on your list and it does not get done, that would be stressful. We don't believe in stress, because that would be unhealthy. Just read it and forget it.

Doing this everyday is a technique for training your brain, training your mind, to bring these priorities to the front of your consciousness. Don't forget that your mind is the most powerful tool you have to make changes in your life. You will slowly be making these things a real part of your everyday life, in a stress-free way. This is the best way to stop "sweating the small stuff" as they say. Soon you will no longer care about your neighbor's barking dog, because it is not a priority to you in the big picture of life. Soon you will not be upset waiting in traffic because it is not important to you in your big picture of life. Soon you will not have road rage at the jerk that just cut you off on the highway, because it is not on your list of things that are important. Soon you will be coming home to your spouse or your friends and you will be talking about the things that are on your list, instead of the idiot who works in the cubicle next to you, because he is not really that important in your big picture of life. Also not important in the big picture of life are your car, your hairdo, your make-up, your jewelry, your gray hairs, or the bird singing outside your bedroom in the morning. You will soon not sweat the small stuff, and these things will no longer cause you stress or ill health. Eventually, without stress and without even trying, you will accomplish number 1 on your "to-do" list. Soon the others will follow, all stress-free, because you want to do them. They have become important to you the right way for the right reasons. Your to-do list will be easy and fun. It will become a game. A game that you will eventually win. In every game there are setbacks. Sometimes the opponent scores. Sometimes you get a little behind in the game. But if you come out ahead four out of seven days a week, then by the end of the month, by the end of the year, you'll be ahead to stay. And you'll stop wasting a lot of time.

"For every minute of anger, you lose 60 seconds of happiness."

Let me relate a little story about my son. I try to teach him these techniques, but he is in high school right now so he knows so much more than I do; at least he says he does. His name is also William. But there are so many "Bills" in my family that we decided to call him "Will" for short. He started taking up the sport of fencing when he was 13. It is a great sport, but there is a lot of thinking and strategy involved. Plus it is a one-on-one sport that is judged by a referee, so there is lots of room for stress because all eyes are on you at all times. It is very frustrating when calls don't go your way, especially when you, and most of the people watching, agree that it was a bad call by the judge. Well my son got into this sport and stuck with it, something he has rarely done in the past. The only thing he ever stuck with in the way of sports was karate. Martial Arts is another one-on-one sport that takes planning, thinking, and strategy. It's another sport that, when competing in a tournament, just like fencing, requires the decision of a judge or referee. All other sports Will tried, and he tried them all, he gave up after one season or less. I think his karate experience (he is a black belt) has helped him a lot in his fencing. He was used to one-on-one competitions. He was used to being watched by a crowd. He was used to being judged, and he was used to the bad calls. But soon in his fencing career he reached a plateau where he did not seem to be advancing as fast as he should. In fact, some competitors that he was defeating regularly were now defeating him. The more he got nervous, the worse he did. The more he worried about it, the worse he did. Then one night it happened:

In a fencing match you try to get your sword or "blade" to touch the other opponent to score a point. The first one to score 15 points or "touches" wins and moves on. The loser is out. One night Will made it all the way to the final match or bout as they are called. The winner would be the champion of the tournament and also get to raise his national ranking. It started out o.k., but when the other fencer landed a few more touches than he did, and a few bad calls did not go my son's way, the stress started to set in. It got worse and worse until all of a sudden the match score was 12 to 3 against my son. His opponent needed only to score three more touches to win, while Will had to score 12 touches to win. Against a good opponent, this was next to impossible. So Will thought about it for a second and decided, "Well I'm not going to win anyway; it would be impossible, so why stress it. I'll just take a deep breath and forget about it, and go out there and try to have some fun and maybe learn from the experience" He continued the bout with his new stress-free attitude and reeled off 12 touches in a row, winning the bout 15 to 12, winning the Tournament and raising his national ranking. He now is an accomplished fencer and is leaving those other fencers who used to beat him way behind. As I write this book he is in his senior year in high school and is, so far, undefeated at the high school level.

More importantly, Will learned something from that one experience (hopefully). Stress, pressure, and worry never really help you become better at anything. They are unhealthy thoughts that decrease your performance, in fencing, and in life. Life is a game of sorts, and some days you win and some days you lose, but it is seldom worth getting sick over. So make your lists, but don't stress over them. Make the list fun. Make it a game. If you don't get everything you want, so what; at least you got to play. And it is a whole lot better than always coming home and talking about the idiot who works next to you, or wishing demise to the neighbor's barking dog. And the reality is, if your list is a list of worthy, positive, achievable goals, you will get them, eventually.

Another truth about health is that if you can control and reduce your stress, you will increase your health, guaranteed.

A final word about the small stuff. Here is a true story that may help demonstrate priorities. It's about time management. You know how I feel about time. Well, there was an expert in time management who was speaking to a group of business students at a prestigious university who used this demonstration to drive home his most important point:

In front of this group of high-powered overachievers he said; "Time for a quiz." He took a one- gallon wide mouth glass jar and filled it with large rocks about the size of a baseball. He carefully placed them in the jar one at a time. When he had no rocks left and the jar seemed like it was filled to the top with no more room for another rock, he asked, "Is the jar full?" Everyone in the class said "Yes."

He then took out a bucket of gravel, put some in the jar, and shook it, so the gravel would work its way down in between the rocks. He then asked again "Is the jar full?" This time many of the students answered, "No, probably not." "Good," he said. He reached out under the table and pulled out a bucket of sand. He started dumping sand in the jar and it went into all the little spaces between the rocks and gravel. Once more he asked if the jar was full. The class shouted "No!" He then got a pitcher of water from under the table and started to pour it in the jar carefully. He filled it to the brim. Now the jar was full. He looked at the class and asked "What is the point of this demonstration?"

One person raised his hand and said "The point is no matter how full you think your schedule is, if you try really hard you can still fit some more things in it!"

"No" the expert said. "Could you get the same amount of materials in the jar if you did it in reverse order: water, then sand, then gravel, then rocks?"

They answered, "No, you could not get as many big rocks in if you tried to put them in last."

The truth this illustration teaches us is:

"If you don't put the big rocks in first, you'll NEVER get them in at all!"

What are the big rocks in your life that you need to fit into your life regularly?

What are your "Big Rocks?" Your children... Your Family... Your health... Your education... Your dreams... A worthy cause... Teaching others... Time for yourself... Your spirituality...

These are the big rocks of your life.

Remember to put these Big Rocks into your life regularly, or you will never get them in at all. If you sweat the little stuff (the gravel, the sand), then you'll fill your life with little things that you worry about, but that don't really matter compared to the big stuff, and you'll never have the real quality time you need for the important things, the "Big Rocks" of your life.

Please reflect on this short story in the near future, and ask yourself: What are the "Big Rocks" in my life? Then, put those in your jar first! Do you have your health? Do your children have their health? Your other loved ones? How can you enjoy the important things in life without your health? Don't wait for it to go away. Put health near the top of your list of priorities. Without health, your entire list of priorities changes, and becomes harder to achieve.

This topic of stress is definitely worth more reading and research on your part. Dr. Hans Selye, M.D., has written many books on stress, and his books are the absolute best place to start. They are all highly recommended, but start with the one called *The Stresses of Life*. He is one of the world's leading medical authorities on stress physiology. I promise you'll learn a lot. For now, try the techniques that I described above; they will at least help organize your stress and may enlighten you as to what is really important in your life. If you can chip away at all of the "small stuff" you will be way ahead of the game. You will be able to handle the bigger stress much more easily, and you will actually be healthier in the process.

> *Start by doing the necessary, then the possible, then suddenly, you are doing the impossible...*
>
> St. Francis of Assisi

Chapter 6
Chiropractic 101

"First they laugh at you, then they ridicule you, then they beat you, then you win!"

Gandhi

Trust that still inner voice that says, "This might work, I'll give it a try..."

I can't let another chapter go by without explaining chiropractic in a little more detail. I know there are still a few doubters out there. Unfortunately you have been listening to the local neighborhood M.D. who told you not to go to a chiropractor unless you have back pain. Remember the corner M.D. that my mother worked for, who I mentioned in chapter 1?

Or maybe your M.D., or friend or neighbor, told you even worse information. I promise that I will again only present scientific facts that I know to be true based on the current available scientific research. Especially in this chapter, especially on this subject, I have learned that I can only present scientific facts and nothing else, because this is a topic that some people still find controversial for some reason. This is a very important chapter to learn and study. If you have gotten this far in the book, you are to be commended. The facts here will be at least interesting to you. Some of this chapter will amaze and astound you (I hope). Either way, I hope you will remember what I first taught you in chapter one: *If anyone says anything different than the information you read here, always ask them, "Where did you read that and can I get a copy?"*

Also remember that you should do some further investigation on the subject if you want to confirm what you learn here, or if you want to expand your knowledge even more.

First, another story:

<u>What kind of medical doctor raises two chiropractors?</u>

Dr. Tony Kennard, M.D., had a son and a daughter who attended New York Chiropractic College. Dr. Kennard's medical credentials and experience are impressive. Dr. Kennard attended school at the London

University Medical School. He first specialized in surgical tuberculosis and then his emphasis shifted to amputee medicine. Dr. Kennard's life found him in the middle of some historically significant events. In 1939 he worked in the British Admiralty War Room, under the watch of Winston Churchill and General Montbatten. He also worked in the Citadel, which was the building that housed the famous "Enigma Machine," the top-secret device that decoded messages from Hitler and his armed forces. Dr Kennard helped chart the invasion of North Africa. In 1942 he flew reconnaissance aviation for England. He was one of the pilots responsible for protecting all of British and American shipping. He also flew Beau Fighters, which were small twin engine airplanes. By the end of the war he had traveled to 33 countries. Medical school followed after the Air Force.

Dr. Kennard witnessed chiropractic first hand as he worked with paraplegics and tuberculosis patients. He noticed that the patients who were being treated by chiropractors were getting the most relief. He began to send all his patients for chiropractic treatment. In fact, his own wife suffered from rheumatoid arthritis and it got so bad that the medical experts there gave up on her. It was only the chiropractor who brought her relief. The whole family began chiropractic treatment. His daughter Tamara participated in competition diving, and the chiropractic treatment relieved her ligament and joint pain without any drugs. Dr. Kennard himself walked with a bad limp for years due to a cycle accident. The chiropractor treated him and since then he walks just fine. Chiropractic treatment was also the only thing that relieved his migraine headaches. His son Ross had always been good with his hands, and when he expressed interest in health care, he thought that skill would be useful in the health care profession. His daughter Tamara also expressed interest in health care, in the area of prosthetics.

Dr. Kennard recognized medicine's role in emergency care, but knew it was not the answer to achieving better health. He knew medicine had to adapt or as he put it "become more human." Dr. Kennard assigns much of the public disillusion with medicine to the profession's *unholy alliance with the pharmaceutical companies*" as he says. Dr. Kennard's son Ross went to New York Chiropractic College and was involved in research there. His daughter Tamara also attended and is now practicing chiropractic in Maine. Dr. Kennard is retired, but still travels whenever he can. So what kind of medical doctor sends his children to become chiropractors? A man whose zeal has attracted a life full of rich moments, whose character demonstrates at every turn a deep and abiding compassion for his fellow man, and a touch of understated heroism. A man with vision and caring for the future of health care.

(This is a true story printed with the permission of NYCC).

Do you remember the end of chapter 3 when we discussed the embryo development? Do you remember the part from *Gray's Anatomy* textbook where it said at about 19 days to 5 weeks a brain and nervous system begins to develop and this layer of nervous tissue maintains connection with all your other body parts? This may be a good time to review that page or two if you don't recall.

One of the very next things to develop is your skeletal system. Bones form around the brain and nervous system to protect it. Around the spinal cord bones form with joints and discs in between them to later allow for movement as well as protection. These will become vertebrae.

The innate intelligence of your developing body is, well, innately intelligent! It has an inborn wisdom. Remember it only takes about nine months to get this extremely complicated and delicate system ready for the world. Once you are born your body is ruled by this brain and nervous system of yours, through an innately intelligent electrochemical relay system inside every nerve cell. Your nervous system picks up signals from the environment and relays the signals to the spinal cord and brain, and they in turn relay messages to your entire body to react appropriately to maintain homeostasis, or health. All you need to do is provide the necessary ingredients to nourish this elaborate system by eating the proper food, and avoid toxins that would poison the system. It will keep working well provided there is no interference.

Albert Schweitzer, M.D., said; *"Each patient carries his own doctor inside him. They come to us not knowing that truth. We are at our best when we give the doctor who resides within each person a chance to work."*

Lewis Thomas, M.D. is quoted saying: *"A kind of super intelligence exists in each of us, infinitely smarter and possessed of technical know-how far beyond our present understanding."*

...and a few thousand similar quotes from other health care experts... All great doctors know this. Few admit it out loud on a daily basis because it may not sound scientific. Based on the information in the first three chapters, you and I know that it actually is scientific. It's that thing that makes human beings much more than just the sum of their parts.

Proper nutrition, exercise, rest and sleep, and keeping low levels of stress will help you avoid the chemical and emotional stress that negatively affect this perfect ecosystem of yours. But what about the physical stress that can affect the communication in your body. What about that thing we have been mentioning called subluxation of your spine for instance? Joints next to your spine, in fact any joint in your body, can misalign slightly. But when it happens to the vertebrae in your spine, it is called *vertebral subluxation*. Let's give vertebral subluxation a good working definition so we know what we mean when we say the word:

Sub means less than, or below the surface. *Luxation* means dislocation. If your shoulder came completely out of joint the medical doctor would diagnose you as having a "luxated" shoulder, or luxation of the shoulder joint. *Subluxation* means less than completely dislocated, but out of proper alignment. When this happens in your spine it is called *vertebral*, referring to the vertebrae, or spinal bone that is out of alignment. When it happens in your spine as opposed to another joint, it can irritate the nerve root that is coming from your spinal cord. This irritation can be from stretching, pulling, or twisting of the nerve, or it can be from pressure on the nerve from muscle/tendon tension, swelling from an injury, aberrant or abnormal joint motion, or lack of proper motion at the joint, and in some extreme cases, if the misalignment is great enough, an actual pinching or touching of the nerve by the vertebrae itself, (or the disc), although this is very rare.

So when most doctors refer to vertebral subluxation, they mean "***a minor misalignment of your vertebrae enough to cause a negative effect on the nerve, and a negative effect on whatever that nerve may go to for proper control.***" That's it, in its most simple terms. That will be our definition of the term "vertebral subluxation" when it is mentioned in this book. There is a longer, five-part definition that includes all the physiology of what happens in the "vertebral subluxation complex" but the stated definition above will do for now. The long-winded scientific definition is in the references at the back of the book and includes the kinesiopathology, myopathology, neuropathology, pathophysiology, and histopathology involved in this condition, and I recommend that any health care providers reading this book should review that information. For the general reader, just know that this condition exists; it is real, proven by science, and it is also very common.

For about a hundred years or so, there seemed to be a lot of controversy about this simple statement. I guess the main reason was that it implies that nerve irritation from the spine could cause organ dysfunction (which it does) and if you remove the nerve irritation, the organ could function better, or at least get a better nerve signal (which it does). But organ dysfunction belonged totally in the realm of the medical doctor. Early on, the medical profession did not want anyone messing with their domain. So they protected their monopoly at all costs. Some of them still try today. Even today you can still find some medical doctors who deter their patients from going to a chiropractor, for fear of losing them as a patient. There are still some medical doctors who never studied chiropractic and so just don't know what it is that we really do. But since their own research now proves what we do is valid, most have come around.

One of many scientific studies by the medical profession itself that proves that the above definition is real and valid comes from the famous "Winsor Autopsies," by Dr. Henry Winsor M.D., from Philadelphia. He knew that many people died of organ failure even if they were being treated by a medical doctor for their condition. Medical treatment depends upon waiting for the organ to begin to fail and cause symptoms, then treating the symptom or organ with drugs. But he finally began to ask the right question. "Why did the organ fail in the first place?" When he noticed that chiropractors were getting better results working with the spine than doctors who were using traditional drug treatments, he planned a research experiment. He dissected human cadavers and animals that died of organ failure. He carried out his famous experiment at the University of Pennsylvania. He did a series of three separate studies. He dissected a total 221 diseased organs. Was there a relationship between the spine and the diseased organs? Here is a quote from his research:

"Of the 221 organs, 212 were observed to belong to the same sympathetic (nerve) segments as the vertebrae in an abnormal curvature... These figures cannot be expected to exactly coincide, for an organ may receive sympathetic filaments from several spinal segments, but in each case there was correlation of the organ to the abnormal spinal segments..."

In other words, Dr. Winsor found almost 100% correlation between minor spinal problems and the corresponding organs that failed. Wow! These insights were prophetic at the time. Since then similar studies by many scientists have expanded upon these findings. This field is one of the fastest growing areas of research in health care, and few can disagree or argue with the consistent findings. Nerves control organs and if the nerve does not work efficiently, the corresponding organ does not work efficiently. The clinical success that chiropractors enjoy thrives on these undeniable scientific facts. Still, for whatever reason, some practicing M.D.'s continue to resist. Most of them at least acknowledge that chiropractors are superior at treating back pain. That's a good start.

One more story that relates the neurological basis of disease.

The true story of Masha and Dasha, conjoined (Siamese) twins joined at the hip and body. The mother of these Russian-born twins was told that they died at birth. The truth was that the Russian medical scientists had them taken to an institution near Moscow for study. They remained there for 20 years. They were born on January 4, 1950. Their interconnection was so extensive that surgical separation would have killed them both. They were unique. They were born with four arms but only three legs. They stand on two legs, one controlled by Masha and one by Dasha. They have separate upper intestines but one shared lower intestine. They have four kidneys but one bladder and often disagree on when to urinate. Their circulatory systems are totally interconnected. So the same bacteria and virus that enters one is automatically present in the other. Yet illnesses affect them differently. Sometimes they get completely different illnesses. (So much for the germ theory of disease). *"I don't like it when they treat us like one person,"* said Masha in a 1989 interview. *"We have one medical record, but we have different illnesses."* Their medical records show Dasha was short-sighted, prone to colds, and right-handed. Masha had a much healthier constitution and had good eyesight, but had high blood pressure. She was left-handed. One became ill with measles but the other did not. This was a mystery to some. The measles virus was in both their bloodstreams and bodies equally; shouldn't both have gotten the measles?

In the 18th century Louis Pasteur claimed that microorganisms caused disease, even in a healthy host. Few medical experts agreed fully, even then. French physiologist Claude Bernard showed that disease would occur only if their host was a suitable candidate. He stated that it was the soil, the terrain, that determined whether or not the bacteria would grow, a fact still supported by science today. He said that microorganisms couldn't cause disease on their own; they need a suitable medium in which to thrive. He was right. Pasteur was wrong, but would not concede the fact until he was on his deathbed, when he said, *"The germ is nothing, the terrain is everything."*

Masha and Dasha share most of their organ systems. They have a common circulatory system, digestive system, excretory system, lymphatic system, endocrine system, skeletal system (they are joined at the hip). But they have separate spines containing separate spinal cords and separate brains. This is the only significant difference between them, and the reason one got measles and the other did not. The unique twins offer an invaluable lesson on the neurological basis of disease, confirming that there is much more to catching measles, or any disease, than simply by taking in the germ. The fact is we take in millions of germs every day, even measles. But we are not always sick. Chiropractors know the fact that the state of your nervous system can affect your immune system and your resistance to disease. Most medical doctors know it too. They are the ones that did the research for us. They just don't like telling you about it.

In 1989, fed up with the mental institution they were forced to live in, the twins staged a protest with the help of some doctors where they were getting some dental work done, and refused to leave to go back to the institution. *"The scientists who took us away did not take into account that we and our mother were human beings, and because of that we have been deprived of family and love,"* Masha said in that 1989 interview. Masha and Dasha became celebrities when they appeared on Russian television. They no longer live in the mental institution. They were united with their mother at the age of 40. (Reprinted with permission of Ted Koren, D.C. *korenpublications.com*.)

So what does this have to do with chiropractic? Everything. Your nerves control your body and chiropractors influence your nervous system. But what does a chiropractor really do? These days many chiropractors specialize in certain areas and so, like medical doctors, not all chiropractors are the same. Some only manipulate necks. Some only manipulate lower backs. Some only treat accident cases. Some only treat athletes. Others specialize in treating infants. What most chiropractors are trained to do is to examine your spine, try to find vertebral subluxations, and then adjust the subluxation into a better position to correct the spine in that area, and, therefore, restore better nerve function. As we have seen, nerve function is the most important function in your body. Over the years chiropractors became more scientific in their approach, and more specific in their treatment.

When experts started to study what we did and why we did it, an interesting discovery was made. That discovery was that there is no better, no safer, no more efficient way to treat most forms of back pain than to use a specific, hands-on chiropractic spinal adjustment. That is how we came to be known as the back pain doctors. Chiropractors get better results treating back pain than ANY other health care professional. Unfortunately most of the world's population still thinks of us as the back pain doctors. Even though the first formal documented chiropractic adjustment of the spine was not to treat back pain.

Spinal manipulation has been around for over five thousand years. Hippocrates, the father of modern medicine, used it and taught it in ancient Greece. In fact the word "chiropractor" comes from the Greek language. It means "practicing by hand." One of Hippocrates famous quotes is: *"Get knowledge of the spine, for this is the requisite for many diseases."* He lived from 460 to 377 B.C.

The developer of chiropractic was a man named Daniel David Palmer. He lived in Iowa and studied magnetic healing and other forms of natural therapy in the late 1890s. D.D. Palmer moved to Davenport, Iowa, where he opened an office to provide health care to the community. He had great success. The story goes that he worked late into the night and was the last one to leave the building except for the janitor, named Harvey Lillard. Harvey Lillard had been almost completely deaf for 17 years after an accident in which he fell when he exerted himself while in an awkward position. When D.D. Palmer examined him he found what he believed to be a problem with Mr. Lillard's spine. He thought that the vertebrae might be out of its normal place. He pushed on the spot and delivered the first chiropractic adjustment. Lillard's hearing returned suddenly, and chiropractic was born. Unfortunately for Palmer, he thought he had discovered the cure for deafness, and when he could not cure other deaf patients, other doctors of the day condemned him. He did not give up, however, and began to study the spine intently, and the anatomy of the nervous system. Here is a description found in D.D. Palmers own writings:

"Harvey Lillard could not hear the racket of a wagon on the street, or the ticking of a watch. I made inquiry as to the cause of his deafness and was informed that when he was exerting himself in a cramped, stooping position, he felt something give way in his back and he immediately became deaf. An examination showed a vertebrae racked from its normal position. I reasoned that if the vertebra was replaced, the man's hearing could be restored. With this object in view, a half hour's talk, I persuaded Mr. Lillard to allow me to replace it. I racked it back into position by using the spinous process as a lever, and soon the man could hear as before..."

Palmer began to use spinal adjustments to treat many other patients with many other conditions, all with good success. He organized his study of the spine and his manipulation techniques and taught them to his son, B. J. Palmer, who then started the first School of Chiropractic in1929. Frustrated with the barbaric medical practices of that time, many students, including medical doctors, attended the school and it quickly became successful. Now a fully accredited college, Palmer College of Chiropractic still stands in Davenport, Iowa, along with 20 other accredited chiropractic colleges all over the world.

Chiropractors have surpassed all others to become the number one drugless health care profession in the world. Chiropractors have also become the number two health care providers to people, right behind medicine, and the chiropractic profession is growing at a faster rate, percentage wise, than medicine. Maybe that could be one of the reasons for the lingering negativity a few practicing medical doctors still hold against chiropractors. When you quickly become number two, and are chasing number one, then number one gets a little nervous. The AMA (American Medical Association) continues to try to protect their monopoly, and the ACA (American Chiropractic Association) continues to defend chiropractic. The two political organizations disagree and are at odds with each other, and this is the "news" that you hear about in the media. And don't forget who owns the media! The good news is, out in the non-political, or at least less political world, where doctors are actually treating patients instead of sitting on boards and committees, many medical doctors and chiropractors are getting along just fine. There are referrals back and forth between medical doctors and chiropractors all the time. There are literally hundreds of offices around the United States where chiropractors and medical doctors equally share the same office and share the same patients. Many of these doctors are equal partners in the practice. If your medical doctor and your chiropractor really care about the best interest of their patient then they will cooperate fully. They will go out of their way to understand what the other is doing and not get caught up in the political nonsense.

If your doctor, chiropractor, *or* M.D., says anything to deter you from going to either one, then run away from them both. They probably have strong ties to their respective associations and fear for their status in these organizations. It's not that different from Democrats and Republicans arguing about their differences. Then, when an issue comes up that would benefit the people who elected them, they don't vote for it because it is against party lines! Find doctors who care about you and your health. Find doctors who know about other disciplines of health care and respect them. After all, it's your health and your decision, not theirs. Take control of your health. Never take their word for anything. Always ask them, *"Where did you read that and can I get a copy?"*

So let us get back to the chiropractic lesson. What does a chiropractor do and why? Your chiropractor should be performing a very specific and complete spinal exam. If he or she suspects a significant problem then he should probably be taking an x-ray of your spine. He or she should study this x-ray carefully and explain it to you so that you can understand it as well.

The chiropractor should correlate all the information found on examination and on the x-ray together, along with your symptoms, and come up with a specific treatment for the correction of your spine. Then he should be making the necessary correction to the spinal joint in a very specific way that makes sense. If your Doctor of Chiropractic is doing something other than that very specific spinal adjustment, by hand, then he is not practicing chiropractic. There may be nothing wrong with what he is doing; just make sure you know that it is not really chiropractic. Medical doctors sell real estate; that's o.k., but they don't call it medicine. Plumbers sell insurance; that's o.k., but they don't call it plumbing. Chiropractors adjust subluxations. Anything else is, well, something else.

Why is subluxation so important? Subluxation is pandemic in our industrialized societies. Subluxation can be caused by stress, be it physical, chemical, or mental/emotional, not just the physical stress of trauma to your spine. This is significant to note and is documented in the scientific literature. Dr. James L. Chestnut's first book, *"The Scientific validation of the Chiropractic Wellness Paradigm"* is a "must read" for every doctor on earth. In it he cites endless scientific support for the statements made in this chapter, and in other chapters in this book.

The chemical stresses discussed in the next chapter that are causing toxicity in our bodies include junk food, air and water pollution, drugs, alcohol, etc... all of which are part of modern living in developed countries. The mental/emotional stresses previously discussed are also part of everyday life, like work, money, family, mortgage, etc... And of course the physical stress of sitting too long, playing sports, bumps and bruises and accidents and so on, all can lead to the "vertebral subluxation complex." Many times all 3 stresses occur at the same time in combination:

Like sitting in traffic, which is a physical stress, a chemical stress (exhaust fumes), and for many, a mental/emotional stress all at the same time. Excessive sitting and lack of motion causes subluxation and spinal decay (arthritis) by placing your spine in an abnormal position and not allowing full range of motion. This leads to joint fixation and dysfunction, just like excessive sugar leads to tooth decay by stressing the enamel of the tooth. Tooth decay is also pandemic in our society because processed sugar is now found in almost all convenience foods.

Like subluxations, cavities occur without pain and so easily become worse without you knowing it. Both cavities and subluxations can result in a nociceptive neurological signal (Negative or irritating signal causing the stress response). Similarly, you cannot take a drug to correct either a cavity or a subluxation, or the symptoms they can cause, and expect to get a physical correction.

Dr. Bill F. Puglisi, D.C., C.C.W.P.

Your spinal column consists of the 24 movable bones called vertebrae. It articulates, or is joined by a joint, to the base of your skull. It is joined at the bottom by articulation with the sacrum and ileum, or hip bones. Inside the center of these spinal bones or vertebrae, is your spinal cord.

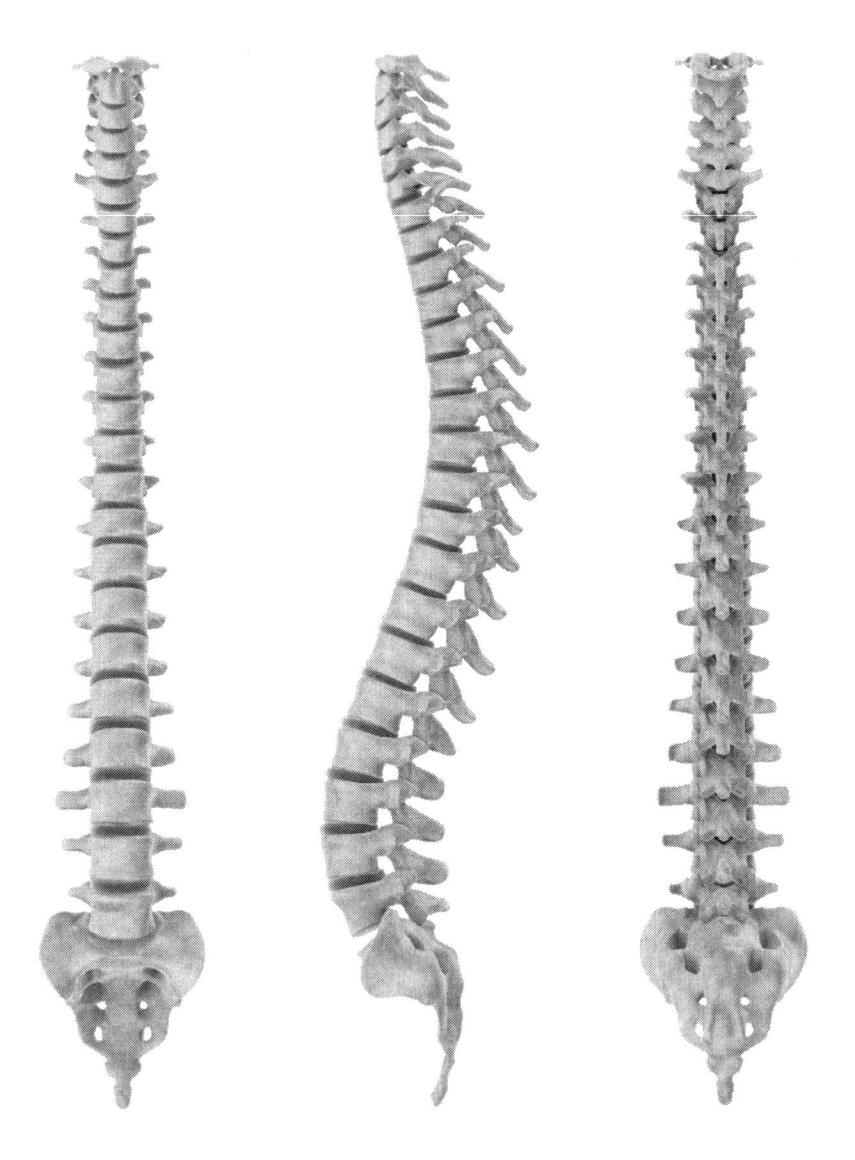

Your Spinal Column

Finally, The TRUTH About HEALTH

Along the course of the spinal cord, as it travels down inside the vertebral column, there are spinal nerve roots that branch out from the cord just like the roots of a tree. They get smaller and smaller as they branch out to go to all the organs and muscles, and every other part of your body. The nerve roots exit the spinal cord at the joints in-between the vertebrae at the level of the discs. Above and below each vertebra there are three joints, a disc plate, and two facet joins, one on each side, above and below, making a total of six joints for each vertebrae.

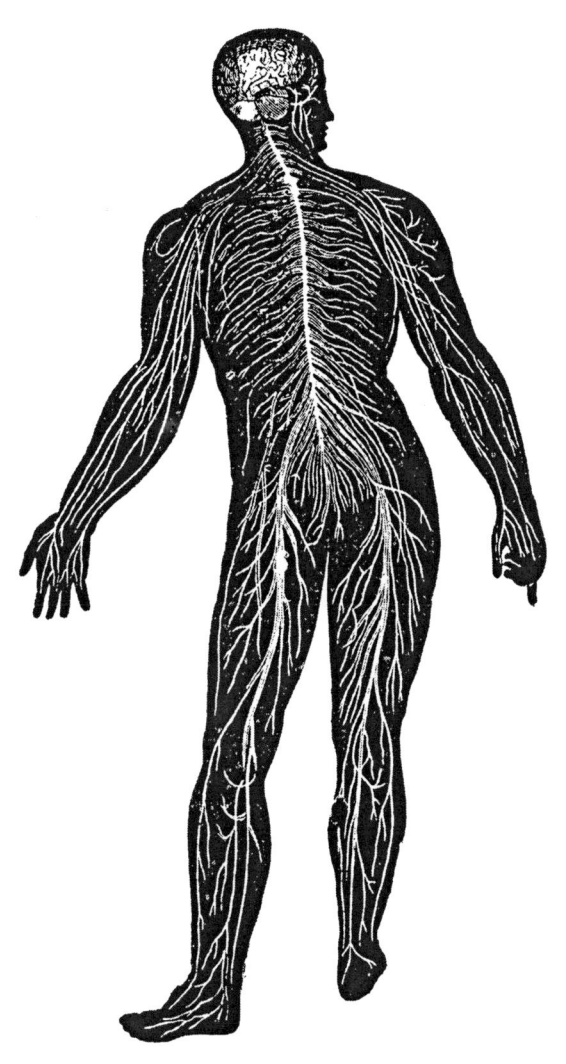

The Spinal Nerve Roots

Dr. Bill F. Puglisi, D.C., C.C.W.P.

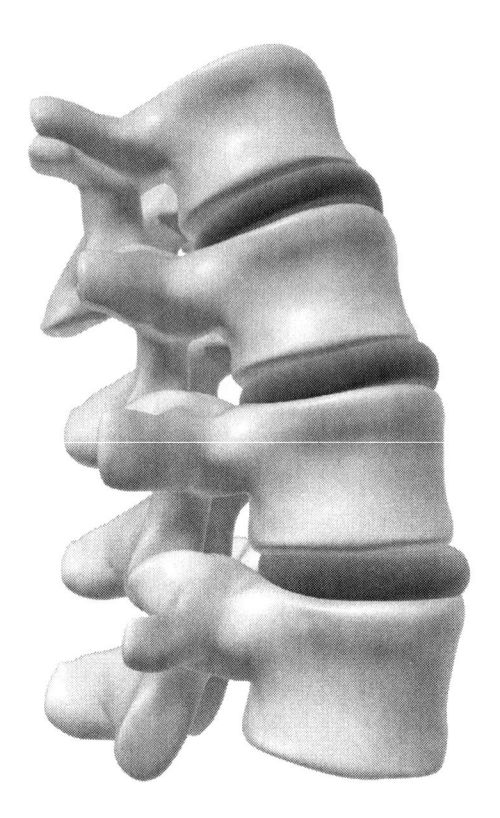

The Spinal Joints

    These joints move individually as you move the center of your body to bend or twist. Remember that any joint can become slightly misaligned, or just get a little stuck and not move properly. This is vertebral subluxation. When this happens to these spinal joints, the improper motion or lack of motion can affect the spinal nerve in a negative way. If this happens then the nerve cells can transmit that "stress response" signal that we previously discussed. This seldom results in significant pain, although it may. In fact, even though only about 10-15% of your entire brain and nervous system is directly sensory, meaning only 10-15% can even feel pain; it is pain that brings most people to a chiropractor. Just keep in mind that if that nerve is causing dysfunction enough to cause pain in your back muscles, then it is also causing dysfunction in whatever else it is going to. The problem is 85% of the rest of your nervous system is not connected to those pain pathways, so the dysfunction can go unnoticed by you. This is a simple anatomical fact, but I will give you an example of what this means. Your stomach is digesting food, but you don't "feel" it. Your diaphragm is contracting, expanding your lungs, but you don't "feel" it. Your arteries are collecting plaque and your heart is starved for blood supply so badly that you are about to have a heart attack and die, but you don't "feel" it. You see, symptoms, especially pain symptoms, are very poor indicators of health.

Another example would be a young Olympic athlete who is on a great diet and exercise program and is at the peak of his performance and health, and then tears up his knee in a competition. He now has lots of symptoms and can barely walk, yet is very healthy internally. Only structure and function together determine health. Only maintaining proper homeostasis and balance in relation to your environment determines the health of the ecosystem that is you. That is what a chiropractor is supposed to help you do, by getting your brain and nervous system to function without any interference from subluxations.

Keep in mind that the chiropractor should keep his main treatment centered on the care and correction of the spine. Anything and everything else should be considered secondary. However, you should also keep in mind that unlike many doctors, your chiropractor is not going to treat you like a part, or a symptom. At least he shouldn't. That would make him a medical doctor. The chiropractor, and all doctors, should always remember that you are a whole person, and as such, you are more than just the sum of your parts. Whatever affects one part of your body effects another part in some way, and everything that happens is in constant communication with your brain and nervous system, whether you feel it or not.

Think of your body as a finely tuned machine. Each part depends on another for optimal performance. Therefore, any doctor that does not have a really good working knowledge of nutrition, exercise, and de-stressing techniques, and does not share proper advice on these topics with his patients, should be brought before his or her respective boards or associations and charged with malpractice. Never allow any doctor to treat you as just a part or a symptom. If you are not treated as a whole person, then simply walk away. There are plenty of chiropractors and medical doctors who care enough to "get it" and are willing to "share it" with those they treat. This is the only way to produce health in a human body that is not functioning at its best. Supply what it needs: proper nerve supply, nutrition, exercise, and love. Then your normal genes will make normal cells that function "normally" to maintain health. That is how any ecosystem is maintained. And that is what you are, an ecosystem.

I have seen many healing miracles in chiropractic. I have seen more scheduled back surgeries cancelled after chiropractic care was tried as a last resort, than I can even count. So many people like Mr. R. B. who came as a last resort to get rid of his back pain, and in the course of treatment not only become pain free after 45 years of suffering, but after practicing my five keys to health program, he was able to stop all his medication as well. Medication for high blood pressure, which he took for 12 years, gone. Medication for diabetes, which he took for 30 years, gone. Medication he took for ulcers for 20 years, gone. All documented conditions in his medical records, yet all symptoms gone with nothing more than following what I say to do in this book.

Many other cases of chronic migraine headaches for years, gone! Many cases like mine, and like Dr. Kennard's wife, where the medical profession gave up, but the healing power of the body was restored when the interference to health was taken away. Yet chiropractors don't perform the miracles. No doctor on earth can really cure you of anything. It is only the healing power of your body itself that can heal you of any condition. Chiropractors don't cure anything, but chiropractors witness more healing miracles than anyone on earth. We just take away the interference to health and let your body take over and do the job it was born to do.

I tell my patients to try this experiment at home to prove this point. I tell them to get a sharp knife and cut one finger on each hand equally. Then take all the medication they have in the medicine cabinet, and put it on the finger of one hand, and wrap it up with their very best band-aids. But on the other finger I tell them to do absolutely nothing. Then I ask them to come back to the office in about 10 days so we can compare the fingers. I bet them that the finger that they did nothing to will be healed just as well as the medicated finger. But who healed the non-medicated finger? The fact is that the medicine did not heal anything. You yourself heal both fingers, medicine or not. No one has ever taken me up on this bet; they usually just take my word for it. Go figure. But if you decide to try it, be sure not to cut yourself so deep that you need stitches! See. There is a place for medical intervention sometimes, in the case of emergencies.

Here is a better analogy. This is a wonderful analogy that I learned from Dr. James Chestnut. The Pond Ecosystem. Dr. James Chestnut contends that health is analogous to light, and sickness is just like darkness. I agree 100%. Sickness is not a real entity; it is just the lack of health. You cannot perform surgery to remove sickness. What does sickness or disease look like? How much does it weigh? What color is it? Sickness or disease is a condition of lack of health. To reduce sickness you must add more health. You cannot surge it out, or drug it out because it is not really there. If there were two adjacent rooms, one dark and one light, with a door between them, what would happen if we opened the door? Would darkness rush into the well lit room making it darker? Of course not. Light is real. Light is an entity that can be measured. Darkness cannot, because it does not really exist, it is just the lack of light, like disease is the lack of health. To get rid of darkness add more light. It is the only way. You cannot drug the darkness away. To get rid of illness, add more health. The next time you get a cold, ask your doctor to surgically remove the cold, but not to remove any body parts.

Think of a pond. What does a pond or small lake need to survive and be healthy? Well, it needs the exact same thing as you do. All the right ingredients for pond health, plus the removal of the toxins that can destroy a pond. First you need sunlight. This is necessary for the plants and algae. You also need plants and algae. A few small fish and frogs and turtles to eat the plants and keep the pond clean. How about a few bigger fish that could thrive on the smaller fish and plants? And what do these fish live in? Water. You would need lots of clean, fresh water. Now construct two ponds in your back yard. Give them both equal amounts of proper pond ingredients for health. Water, sunlight, plants, algae, fish, frogs, turtles, etc. Once complete and thriving, continue to give one pond a clean source of water, and watch it take care of itself, each part of the pond depending on each other part for survival. But to the other pond with the same starting ingredients, add lots of cheeseburgers and fries, ice cream, cake, candy and cookies. Add a touch of runoff from the local city dump. After 10-20 years what do the ponds look like? Is one pond older than the other? Did one pond age faster? No. Is one pond genetically inferior? What drugs will you add to the pond to fix it? What surgery will you perform on the pond to restore health? What defective parts will you remove? The plants? The algae? The sunlight? That makes no sense! The parts of the pond are not defective and do not need to be removed. So why do you do it to the ecosystem that is your body? That is not what a chiropractor would do.

Yet I'm sure there are a few traditional medical practitioners that could show you a small, obscure bias research study done by a drug company that would indicate that drugs or surgery for your pond would be appropriate. In fact they would also argue that there are not enough double-blind scientific studies or experiments conducted that would prove that taking out all the toxins from the pond would restore it to health, even though *common sense* would bring you to that conclusion.

Here is how they would (and do) twist their "scientific study":

The drug company wants to see if vitamin E is beneficial to your heart. So they decide to do an experiment. They take hundreds of already sick people with heart disease who are on a poor diet (which probably caused their heart disease) and divide them into three groups. One group gets vitamin E, the second group gets a placebo, and the third group gets nothing, the "control" group. All three groups keep eating the same crappy diet that causes heart disease. At the end of the "scientific" study each group is tested, and it is found that the group that took vitamin E did not show any improvement in their heart disease. Some even got worse. So the "scientific" conclusion was that vitamin E is not beneficial for your heart! But wait, don't we all know that vitamin E is beneficial for you, and in fact essential for normal function, including heart function? Sure, but that doesn't matter. The double-blind scientific study showed no statistical improvement with or without vitamin E. There is no room for frivolous common sense in a drug company research study. This is not an exaggeration. This is how bias research is done. In fact, this is exactly what happened when a drug company did a recent study on vitamin E. They actually got it published and printed in the news and on TV in 2005.

Help me out with this one: You have a lot of plants in your back yard. Most of them are not doing well, and some are dying, so you decide to do a scientific experiment to determine what is wrong with your plants. So you get some good clean water, and you water all your plants equally. Some do better, but most do poorly, and some die. So your conclusion is that water has no significant benefit to plants. But wait! Don't we know that plants benefit from water? Well our recent scientific study says there is no statistically significant evidence that the plants benefited from water. This is what the conclusion would be from a drug company study. But you don't give up, and you try something else. You notice that some plants are not getting much sunlight. So you move the plants around so that they all get an equal amount of sunlight. Some plants do better, but most do poorly and some die. The scientific conclusion from the drug company would be that sunlight has no measurable benefit to plants. But wait! Don't we all know that plants need sunlight to survive? Not these plants. These plants must have genetically mutated and no longer benefit from sun or water. It must be the genes; what else could it be? But you don't give up, and try again. This time you decide to give a high quality organic plant food to all your plants. After you do, some plants do better, most do poorly, and some die. You bring the results to your drug company to interpret, and they conclude that your plants would not benefit from plant food, or water, or sunlight. The proof is right there in black and white.

But what about common sense? No place for that in a drug study. Why, that would be chiropractic. Take the results of your experiment to your chiropractor and he would (should) say, "Obviously your plants are suffering from some deficiency of a required ingredient for homeostasis, or they are suffering from some type of toxicity in their environment. Instead of just noting the symptoms and treating those, let's examine your plants and their environment and get to the real cause of the problem." After careful inspection of the plants, as a whole, and their environment, it is discovered that your neighbor had been dumping his old motor oil in a hole near your fence, and the toxic oil was leaching into your garden, killing your plants. Fixing this subluxation in your soil will eventually restore your plants to better health.

A chiropractor works from the inside out, allowing your body to express the health that it wants to express, naturally. Much of medicine works from the outside in, covering up the symptoms, thus quieting the body's cry for help. A chiropractor evaluates each patient as a whole person and tries to detect all environmental stressors. At least a Subluxation-Based Wellness-Chiropractor does. Some chiropractors just treat the spine only. They treat the part only. They try to practice traditional medicine by fixing one thing and then ignore the rest of the ecosystem. This is sometimes a mistake, although the results are still pretty good. Even the most average chiropractor gets a success rate of almost 80% with musculoskeletal conditions, like back pain. Most medical doctors are around 50/50. Many medical doctors are now getting the big idea, and are learning the principles in this book and becoming very knowledgeable about nutrition and exercise, and then are advising their patients on these topics. So which is the better system of treatment now, chiropractic or medicine? One is not better than the other. They are different in the basic approach, but if you cover all the bases and finally end up learning how to supply your body with all the ingredients it needs to be healthy, along with learning how to remove all the toxins that are interfering with making you healthy, then you win.

See, it is up to the individual doctor to be complete in his philosophy and his approach. Remember, it is not the doctor who heals you. It is your own body's healing power that heals. The doctor is only there to assist you in removing toxins and adding the healthy required ingredients in an organized way that makes sense. If the job is done right, does it matter who assisted? A chiropractor, a medical doctor, an osteopath, or a circus clown could give you this same advice and get you started on the road to true health. The required ingredients for health are the same for everyone. They have been for almost 50,000 years. The toxins that prevent health are the same for everyone. They have been for thousands of years. Don't get caught up in the fight between traditional medicine and the chiropractic profession. It is not the profession that heals you. It is you who heals you. All you need to do is remove the interference. The only real difference between medical doctors and chiropractors should be that only chiropractors can deliver the very specific spinal adjustment to correct your spine. That is what they are trained to do, that no one else is trained to do. When you are in an emergency situation, a life-threatening situation, then you need the medical doctor and his or her special skills that a chiropractor may not be trained in. There is room for both, side by side, because there is need for both, side by side. We have different specialties, but in the end our concern should only be to help the patient get healthy. I'm not sure where most medical doctors go astray and lose sight of this fact. But know that many chiropractors go astray also, as do osteopaths and circus clowns. Not everyone is perfect. In fact no one is perfect, or better, just different. You should look at it this way:

A good, Subluxation-based, Wellness-chiropractor is the electrical contractor of your body's ecosystem. The medical doctor is the fire department of your ecosystem. Do I hate the fire department? No, in fact, I love the fire department, and I have their number in my phone book in case I need them. You should, too. But I do hate their hoses and axes (drugs and surgery) because if they use them on me I know that my body is in an emergency situation. So if your house is on fire do you call the chiropractor or the fire department? Obviously you call the fire department. They come with their most advanced technology, their very best hoses and axes, and put out your fire. But how does your house look after they have used their hoses and axes; healthy? No, because they have nothing to do with health, they are there for the emergency, they save the house's life. Who do you call when the fire is out? You call the electrician to rewire your house. You call the chiropractor to make your house healthy again. You want the electrician to wire your house so well that you never have a fire. The value in chiropractic is not so much in relieving back pain as much as it is making your house so healthy that you never have a fire. This is the specialty of a Subluxation-Based Wellness-Chiropractor. Not putting out the fire, but PREVENTING the fire. You better believe that I want to have the fire department in my neighborhood, and have their number in my phone book. But I never want to have to call them, do you? I have not been treated by a medical doctor for sickness or disease since I was 3 ½ years old. But if I was in an accident tomorrow, and my leg was severed, I would not ask to be taken to a chiropractor to have it "adjusted" back on. I would want to go to the nearest hospital, get the best doctor available, and have surgery on my leg. I might even ask him to give me lots of drugs before he started the surgery. This is the way you need to think about the difference between chiropractors and M.D.'s. Not as enemies or opposites, but allies in the treatment of your ecosystem.

As mentioned, many medical doctors and chiropractors work side by side already, even in the same office sharing the same patients. This is how it should be. Subluxation-Based Wellness-Chiropractor first, and then a medical doctor for crisis care. There are plenty of ecosystems out there for everyone to treat and help.

This country is in a health crisis. Remember that we are only the 37th healthiest country right now, and dropping. That's because many medical doctors try to do what they do and call it health. They argue that they can use their axes and hoses to keep you healthy. They claim that if they come over to your house every day and wet it down inside and out, that you will not get a fire. They even have some "scientific drug studies" done by biased drug companies that prove that if they wet your house down everyday inside and out, that you won't get a fire. This may be true, but how is your house working after you wet it down inside and out every day? Why would you take the toxic drugs everyday just to prevent the fire? Taking drugs cannot make you healthy. Adding toxic chemicals (remember the LD-50...) cannot produce health. It can only, at best, put out the fire. It's the wrong premise for the argument. The only way to get truly healthy is to remove all the toxins and add more health. I don't want the medical doctor's job, and he should not want mine. Get your spine checked for subluxations by a Subluxation-Based Wellness-Chiropractor; it's the right thing to do. And find a medical doctor who really cares, and knows the facts in this book. They are out there. We are separate and distinct and both are necessary if we are going to save this country from the drug companies and the fast food franchises that are both going out of their way to keep us sick.

Just in case you think that medical doctors are all against chiropractors, and just in case you don't bother to read the references in the back of the book to support the facts in this chapter, I thought I would include here, what the medical experts, the big guys, are saying about chiropractic:

Dr. Ralph DeNagy, M.D., a research scientist and medical doctor who has been part of five Nobel-prize-winning research teams says in his research *"interference to the nervous system results in permanent damage in a very short time period, therefore chiropractic care should begin at birth and continue on a preventative basis."* This is one the leading neurologists on the planet telling you to get to a chiropractor, just like he himself does on a regular basis.

Abraham Tobin M.D., a Harvard medical school professor and researcher, states that *"Infant subluxation is so wide spread, stressing the nervous system, that chiropractic care should begin as early as possible and continue throughout life."* This is the best of the best medical doctors, telling you to get chiropractic care now, no matter what your symptoms.

Speaking of the best of the best, over **2000** Harvard Medical School doctors are now under regular chiropractic care, and recommending it to you. Why would you listen to a local M.D. who probably knows little or nothing about it, when he says not to go to a chiropractor unless you have back pain, or not to go at all?

Dr. Zeanith H. Stamets, M.D., author of *Cancer Research and Treatment and Allied Diseases"* states that *"along with any other treatment you may be getting, chiropractic adjustments of the spine are **required** to restore normal functions which are lost due to medical treatments, especially cancer treatments."* Another leading expert saying that everyone who has received medical treatment needs chiropractic treatment, especially cancer patients.

Dr. Leon Chaittow M.D., DO, DN, a doctor and author of the book *A World Without AIDS* strongly recommends that: *"upon receiving a serious diagnosis such as AIDS, the person should begin and maintain regular chiropractic care, along with other natural methods that are proven, like chiropractic, to strengthen your immune system."*

The **Sloan-Kettering Institute for Cancer Research** did a study that showed that people under chiropractic care had immune systems that tested **200-400% stronger** than the average person who was not under chiropractic care, another undeniable fact from a medical authority, supporting the value of chiropractic care for everyone. It's not just about the back pain.

Dr. William D. Kelley, DDS, an orthodontist who successfully treated his own cancer, now uses his program to help others overcome cancer, and other supposedly "incurable diseases," recommends to all his patients to *"receive regular chiropractic care the entire time they are following my program, and then continue afterwards for preventative maintenance."*

Dr. L. Guttmann M.D., a famous and respected German medical doctor, found in his research that *"blocked nerve impulses from the atlas, (the first bone in your spine), causes many clinical problems from central motor impairment, lower resistance, infections, especially ear, nose, and throat infections."* He clearly states that, *"Chiropractic care can bring about amazing results because the treatment is a causal one."* He concluded that *"approximately 80% of all children are not in autonomic nerve balance and many have this atlas subluxation and should be checked by a chiropractor."* (A Subluxation-Based Wellness-Chiropractor)

Dr. Ronald Pero M.D., Ph.D., Ph.D. in toxicology and a toxicologist researcher, found in his study that: *"**Subluxation decreases the genetic potential of human beings.**"* i.e., Nerve irritation from subluxation changes the expression of our genes! This bold statement is actually confirmed by many scientific researchers in the field of quantum physics, and other experts like **Bruce Lipton, Ph.D.** in cellular biology, medical school professor, and author of *The Biology of Belief*. Remember the chapter on genes and this one actually becomes obvious to us now.

Dr. G.W. Raby, M.D., *"I do not practice medicine anymore. Chiropractic is a lot better. I can reach more cases and go more directly to the cause of the disease by chiropractic than I can by medicine, and do it better and more scientifically."*

Alfred Walton, M.D., *"Chiropractic reaches successfully a large number of so-called chronic diseases more than any other known method, and is so much superior to the drug method that it is truly laughable to compare them."*

E.W. Fiege, M.D., *"I have seen the results of these chiropractic methods... that have never been obtained by anything taught in medical college, and never can be until they come to their senses and teach these methods they now condemn."*

W.E. Brayman, M.D., *"For 20 years I practiced medicine, not satisfied with the results of my work. I investigated chiropractic... I got satisfactory results, something I could not have done under medical procedures. It makes me feel like shouting hurrah for chiropractic."*

William A. Seeley, M.D., *"I started out...to conquer the demon 'disease' with drugs. I too often failed, as they all do... the more I studied and experimented, the more I was convinced that the real cause of disease was impinged nerves, and that chiropractic adjustment was the most scientific way to release them. Results are what count and chiropractic care when scientifically given brings them."*

U.A. Lyle, M.D., *"I believe chiropractic to be the most scientific method of removing the cause of disease, thereby allowing nature to resume normal action, which effects the recovery of the patient from bodily ailments."*

Frederick L. Fischer, M.D., *"I could not help but see this wonderful new light, and today in my practice of chiropractic, I walk into the sick room with absolute confidence that I have, in chiropractic, complete control over disease. I no longer believe that a drug will do the work..."*

Windsor Autopsies. As previously mentioned, Dr. Henry Windsor, M.D., a famous surgeon and pathologist, helped to prove chiropractic validity by doing autopsies on people who died of organ failure. He wanted to find out why the organs failed, even when treated by doctors. He stated: *"EVERY organ that failed that was related to the death of the patient was linked to a corresponding nerve root at the spinal level. There was virtually a 100% correlation linking spinal problems with organ dysfunction."*

Archives of Internal Medicine. In an insurance survey review study, it was found that *"people with chiropractic insurance coverage were hospitalized 41% less often than those without."*

What more support can you give than that? Well actually, a lot. I could fill this book with similar quotes. Please read the references in the back if you have a chance. The truth is out: Chiropractic is real, it's valid, it's scientific, it's recommended by the best of the best medical doctors, and it works! Don't forget the fact that NO ONE TREATS BACK PAIN MORE EFFICIENTLY than a chiropractor. NO ONE! It's cheaper, it's safer, and it works better than any other treatment, one of those undeniable scientific facts that no one could argue.

On occasion I have been addressed on the subject of safety. So in case there is any doubt still left, I will relate the safety issue to you. People sometimes say "I don't want anyone to 'crack' my neck." To that I say, "Good, then you should go to a chiropractor. Chiropractors, Subluxation-Based Wellness-Chiropractors, do not "crack necks." Chiropractors specifically and carefully "adjust" the joint between bones for better alignment. Occasionally this movement of the joint causes a sound. Bones do not touch other bones. All bones in your body are separated by a joint. The joint noise that you sometimes hear in your ankle, wrist, or neck when you move them, is the same sound you hear when you pop your knuckles, or when you get an adjustment by a chiropractor. Millions of chiropractic adjustments are given every day to infants and children and elderly, and everyone in between. The incidence of a negative effect is almost nonexistent. To ease your mind even further, here are some interesting facts and statistics.

Chiropractic Education and Medical Education Compared:

	Chiropractic class hours	Medical school hours
Anatomy	540	508
Physiology	240	326
Orthopedics	210	156
Obstetrics	60	148
Psychiatry	60	144
Radiology	360	148
Neurology	324	112
Diagnosis	630	324
Microbiology	120	114
Chemistry	165	325
Pathology	360	401
Total hours	3,069	2,706
Based on the review of the average professional college curriculum in the U.S.A.		

Clearly chiropractors are among the best trained health care professionals in the country, and in the world.

Also, insurance companies do extensive research into the areas of safety. That is their job: to evaluate the safety of a situation and then write insurance policies based on the safety level of that situation. Chiropractors in every state have some of the lowest premiums among all health care professionals for liability insurance policies. They are only a fraction of what most medical doctors pay. Insurance companies know that chiropractic is safe.

Here are some risk ratios that may interest those concerned about serious side effects.

Actual incidence of stroke in the general population:		
Surgery for neck pain	1 in 10,000	= .0001% stroke (many other complications)
Chymopapin injection	1 in 700	= .014% stroke (many other side effects)
Medical anesthesia	1 in 100	= .1% stroke (many other serious effects)
Balloon Angioplasty	9,000 deaths per year	= .009% deaths from stroke
Bypass surgery	28,000 per year	= .4% stroke (many more deaths not from stroke)
Angiogram tests	4,500 deaths	= .005% by stroke (other deaths not due to stroke)
Going for a haircut	3 in 100,000	= .00003% die from stroke
Non-chiropractic cervical manipulation	10 in 100,000,000	= .00000001% stroke
Chiropractic manipulation	3 in 165,000,000	= .0000000012% stroke
***Spontaneous stroke, no known cause**	3 in 100,000 of all strokes	= .000003%
According to the *New England Journal of Medicine*		

The incidence of stroke is also much higher for other activities such as exercise, Tai Chi, falls, medical stress tests, almost all medical tests, massage, and *any* head turning event! All studies ever reviewed related to stroke show that the risk is far greater after being treated by a medical doctor than by a chiropractor, but these studies are never cited in the *"popular news"* sources according to Dr. Alan Tarrot, M.D., a medical researcher. He states in his research reviews that:

"Chiropractic manipulation" is the term used all the time when reporting *any* adverse event, even though *"...the manipulation was rarely done by a trained chiropractor, but usually by an untrained medical doctor, physical therapist, message therapist, or high school wrestling coach. The reporting is simply bias against chiropractors"*

Look at those statistics above carefully. Not only is EVERY medical procedure you can think of more likely to cause a stroke than a chiropractic neck adjustment, but you are more likely to have a spontaneous stroke* from no known cause than to have one from a chiropractic adjustment. This means that **people under chiropractic care actually have a lower incidence of stroke than the general population of people** not under chiropractic care! I hope this eases the minds of any doubters out there. Chiropractors do not cause strokes, period. You are more likely to have a stroke if you don't go to a chiropractor, than if you do.

Sometimes testimonials carry as much weight as scientific studies for some people. Well, almost every major entertainer in Hollywood that you can think of is under chiropractic care. These are millionaires who can choose any type of care they want without consideration of insurance policies, and they choose chiropractic first. Great entertainers like Cher and Madonna, and countless others, choose chiropractic first, and credit their chiropractors for their ability to keep up with their grueling schedules.

Almost every major athlete you can think of is under chiropractic care. More chiropractors went to the last Olympic Games with the U.S. Olympic team than did medical doctors. Many athletes will not compete in their sport without a chiropractic adjustment first, like Evander Holyfield, Joe Montana, Bruce Jenner, and many others. I saw a friend of mine, Dr. Nick Athens, DC, adjust Joe Montana on national TV just before the San Francisco 49ers won the Super Bowl in the 1980s. In fact, recently Tiger Woods and Lance Armstrong both credited their chiropractor with helping them achieve their level of success. Most professional sports teams now have a chiropractor on their staff. Another great success story is Bo Jackson. Bo Jackson, for those of you who may not remember, was a pro football player and a professional baseball player. He suffered from a severely injured hip while playing football, and was told by his medical experts that his sports career was over.

Well, Mr. Jackson found a chiropractor to help him, and was able to recover well enough not only to play sports, but he actually returned to professional baseball, and played for the Kansas City Royals. He credited his chiropractor with his amazing come-back.

Over 200 million families of all ages, over 500 million people worldwide, now use the high-performance healing of chiropractic on a regular basis. Based on the facts presented in this chapter, maybe Subluxation-Based Wellness-Chiropractic care is something that you should try, or at least investigate further.

To end this chapter, here is a quote taken directly from B.J. Palmer who started the first College of Chiropractic:

The Big Idea

"A slip or fall produces a subluxation. The subluxation is a small thing.

The subluxation produces pressure on a nerve. That pressure is a small thing.

That decreased nerve flowing produces a diseased body. That is a big thing to that man.

Multiply that sick man by a thousand, and you control the physical and mental welfare of a city.

Multiply that man by one hundred thirty million, and you forecast the physical and mental status of a nation.

So the slip and fall, the subluxation, pressure, flow of mental images and disease, are big enough to control the thoughts and actions of a nation.

Now comes a man, and one man is a small thing.

The man gives an adjustment. The adjustment is a small thing.

The adjustment replaces the subluxation. That is a small thing.

The adjusted subluxation releases pressure on the nerves. That is a small thing.

The released pressure restores the man to health. This is a big thing to that man.

Multiply that well man by a thousand, and you step up the physical and mental well-being of a city. Multiply that well man by a million and you increase the efficiency of a state.

Multiply that well man by a hundred thirty million, and you have produced a healthy, wealthy, and better race for posterity.

So the adjustment of the subluxation to release pressure upon nerves, to restore mental impulse, to restore health, is big enough to rebuild the thoughts and actions of the world.

The idea that knows the cause, that can correct the cause of disease, is one of the biggest ideas I know. Without it nations fall. With it nations rise.

This idea is the biggest I know of.
B.J. Palmer 1944

Chiropractors, just like medical doctors, don't actually heal anything, but I can assure you that chiropractors, by improving nervous system function, do witness more healing miracles than anyone else on earth.

> *"There are only two way to live your life. One is as though nothing is a miracle. The other is as though everything is a miracle."*
>
> *Albert Einstein*

Chapter 7

...but what do I eat?

"Give a man a fish, and feed him for a day. Teach a man to fish and feed him for a lifetime."

And now the moment you've all been waiting for, the nutrition chapter. Why is nutrition always the hottest topic of discussion in natural health care? Well it seems that here, more than anywhere else, is where false information about health abounds. There are hundreds, maybe thousands, of diet and nutrition books out there, all saying something different! Can they all be right? Can they all be wrong? Well, all I can say about that fact is, America has more and more diet and weight-loss books every year, and America gets more and more obese every year. Heart disease, stroke, and cancer are on the rise, and in most cases they are directly related to what you are eating. One of the problems is that the authors of those books confuse weight-loss with health. Sure it's healthier in general to be at a proper body-fat content. But just losing weight is not enough to be healthy. The fact is you and I could eat nothing but one chocolate milkshake everyday and lose weight. But would doing that make us healthy? Of course not, in fact we would become even less healthy if we did. So you and I could also lose lots of pounds on a weight-watching diet that includes white bread, prepared processed foods, and desserts with sugar substitutes. But we would still get diabetes, liver disease, and kidney disease directly from that diet. We would just look a lot better as we were killing ourselves. And so it is with MOST of the popular diets currently on the market. Actually, I hate the word "diet." There is a better way.

The TV commercials have been able to engrain "the big lie" into you so well that when you hear the truth, it seems controversial. Remember how I started the book by mentioning milk? I bet you're still upset about that, aren't you. We are going to expose a lot of health myths in this chapter. This is one of my favorite chapters in the book, maybe because the changes people make after learning this information result in the biggest difference in their health. Maybe it's because of the controversy over the subject. Maybe it's because it is a direct attack on the huge fast-food industry, which is like the story of David and Goliath, only tenfold. But I think it's my favorite because I'm from that big old-fashioned Italian family that I talked about.

Food was important in my family. At certain times, like the holidays, it is by far the most important thing in life, more important than life itself! Everything centers on the food. Meals are planned weeks in advance of Thanksgiving and Christmas. It is a huge operation taking many days and many people. The meal is extravagant and lasts for hours. I can still remember just the regular Sunday dinners at Grandma's house. It started the day before, when my aunt would come over to Grandma's to help make the home-made pasta from scratch. My grandmother cooked three meals a day seven days a week for as long as I could remember. Nothing came from a can or a box. She would cook breakfast, lunch, and dinner from scratch. When I was kid my grammar school was closer to her house than my own, so I went there almost every day. I would usually sleep at my Grandma's house more than I would sleep at home during the school year. Other than being with my dad on the weekends, the next closest adults that I spent time with when I was young were my grandparents, Angie and Nick. My grandmother was from Italy. My grandfather, Nick, was from Brooklyn, NY, at that time pretty much the same thing as being from Italy. They both cooked... a lot.

My grandfather cooked for the neighborhood deli. My grandmother cooked for everyone else. In those days, they let grammar school kids go home during lunch hour. There was no cafeteria in most schools. I would go to Grandma's. There was always a hot meal waiting for me there every day. After school I would go there to do my homework and eat supper. Then I would go to my friend Joe's house; he lived only a few houses away. I never went there on an empty stomach. Grandma and Grandpa are gone now, but it's still about the food in my family. If you ever saw the movie *My Big Fat Greek Wedding*, then you know what I'm talking about. It's exactly the same in an old-fashioned Italian family as it is in an old-fashioned Greek family.

My grandmother taught me how to cook. I helped her prepare a lot of meals. She never measured anything, and everything always came out perfect. There was never any waste, and nothing ever got thrown away. I loved those old days and I miss them, especially the food. But I came to find, in school and in my research, that the food we ate was not always the healthiest. Of course it was way better for you than anything you can get in any restaurant anywhere in the present day. And it tasted better too, mostly because it was made with love, which is usually as important, if not more important, than the actual ingredients. We sat down, all together, and took our time to eat. We would talk. We would eat some more. And we would talk some more. Then we would usually eat some more. We were surrounded with love, and that was one of the things that made it healthy. Remember that your state of mind is just as important in being healthy as anything else. With that in mind, please remember there is research, and common sense in everything I am about to say. I could write forever just on nutrition and not cover it all. But for here, I will try to keep it as short and simple as possible. After you get these basics, do further research on your own to learn more.

We need to eat the way we are genetically designed to eat. We need to eat the way our ancestors have been eating for the last 40,000 years or so. We need to eat the things that our digestive systems have adapted to processing into the basic carbohydrates, proteins, and fats that our body uses. We need to take in the vitamins, minerals, and water to assist in that process. And that's it. All our bodies need to thrive are carbohydrates, fats, protein, vitamins, minerals, and water. Anything else is a stress to your digestive system and to the rest of your body, since it was not available 5,000 to 50,000 years ago. Our digestive system is designed only to eat what was available during that time.

Here is the basic list of foods that you should eat, and why:

Eat green leafy vegetables.

Why?

There is no healthier food on the planet. Guaranteed! Make green vegetables part of your meals everyday. Without them you cannot be healthy, period. They contain a perfect balance of vitamins, minerals, and fiber that sustain life. I find it amazing how many people do not eat at least some vegetables every single day. This is one of the easiest ways to get healthier almost immediately.

Eat almost any other vegetables, except white potatoes. Why?

Almost all vegetables are good for you in their natural state. Vegetables contain the vitamins and minerals you need to live on. They also contain the fiber that you need for a healthy digestive system. It is hard to find vegetables that are not good for you. They simply must be part of your daily diet for life. Potatoes are one of those few vegetables that are the exception. White potatoes have a high "glycemic index." This means they get turned into sugar by your digestive system. Their starchy carbohydrates turn into sugar rather quickly and clog up and even destroy insulin receptors on your cells, just like white sugars and refined, processed grains do. Also, conventionally grown white potatoes are one of those foods that are heavily treated with toxic chemicals. Did you know that just a few states in the Northwest U.S. are suppliers of 80% of the white potatoes in the entire world? Did you know that most of these farms use fertilizer that contains heavy metal poisons and toxic waste byproducts from the steel industry? Read the book *Fateful Harvest* by Duff Wilson if you want to know how most of your big industrial farmers grow their food. If you must have a white potato, then please only buy organic, and keep them to a minimum. It would be best to eliminate them all together, especially since white potatoes are usually eaten with meat. The digestive chemicals needed to digest meat are the opposite of those needed to digest potatoes. In your stomach they tend to cancel each other out and so neither the meat nor the potato is digested properly. This adds to gastrointestinal problems.

Eat fruits. Almost any vine-ripened organic fruit, with the exception of some melons, can be consumed in almost any quantity. Why?

Again fruit has the vitamins and minerals that you need, and the fiber that you need to be healthy. Melons, however, have a low nutritional value per gram, and also a high glycemic index, like white potatoes. Most melons are fine to consume in small quantities. Just don't enter the watermelon-eating contest at the summer picnic. A small quantity means less than a 1-cup serving a few days per week, or less.

Eat eggs. Yes that's right, EGGS ARE GOOD FOR YOU! You can eat two to three eggs a day, four to six days a week and be fine. But be careful here too. Only organic, free-range eggs are healthy. If your eggs are not organic, limit them to two or three eggs per week. Preferably raw or minimally cooked. Why?

Eggs are a good source of protein, B vitamins, essential amino acids, and the "good" form of cholesterol. But cooking destroys the enzymes and also binds the proteins making them more difficult to digest than raw or partially cooked eggs. The less they are cooked, the better. Organic eggs are fine raw, like in your salad dressing, but if you are eating conventionally raised, non-organic eggs, cook them a little because of the rare possibility of salmonella contamination.

Eat Fish. Non-carnivorous, ocean-caught fish only.

Why?

First of all, because of toxic buildup over time called "bio-accumulation." Big fish eat little fish. The bigger and older the fish is, the higher the levels of mercury, pesticides, PCB's and other poisons. Farm-raised fish is 50 to 100 times worse than ocean-caught fish, because they are raised with 50 to 100 times more chemicals, and because of their controlled diet has little or no omega-3 fatty acids, which is the main reason to eat fish in the first place. Farm-raised fish are raised in crowded and dirty conditions, often in pools or vats with poor filtration or chemical filtration. The toxic buildup is tremendous. There are many articles and studies about how bad and unhealthy farm-raised fish are compared to ocean-caught wild fish. Farm-raised salmon, for example, has a dull, gray flesh. So they put chemical dye in the food and water to make it look orange like ocean salmon. Check the back of the book for references. Remember that the ocean is polluted too, so keep your fish consumption down to once or twice per week, at most. The smallest fish, like anchovies, sardines, and herring are the healthiest, least polluted fish, so they can be eaten in larger quantities.

Eat nuts and seeds. Preferably fresh and raw. Buy them whole, unpeeled, and still in the shell if possible. Why?

Nuts and seeds are an excellent source of protein and fatty acids and even some fiber. They are among the healthiest things to eat if you eat them raw. But air and light oxidizes the oil in most nuts and seeds and so turns them rancid very quickly. Cooking them also destroys most of their nutritional value, although they are still healthy if cooked, just not as nutritious as raw ones. Store them in a cool dark place, and eat them soon after you buy them.

Eat sprouts. Organic sprouts should be eaten daily.

Why?

Sprouts are a great, clean, fiber-rich, nutrient-dense food packed with vitamins and minerals. Remember, they are about to become a vegetable. Top off your salads with fresh sprouts whenever you can. Try all different varieties. Mix them together. Also it's easy and fun to grow your own. Just buy the beans or seeds and put them in a big glass jar. No dirt necessary. Just add a little water and put them in a dark place, and in only a week you will have fresh sprouts.

Eat (certain) meat. I bet you didn't think I was going to say that! It turns out that some meat is o.k. to add to a healthy-eating lifestyle. Eat meat sparingly. Eat ONLY organic, GRASS FED, free range, hormone-free, pesticide-free, unprocessed, lean meat.

Why?

Humans were meant to eat meat, according to the design of our digestive systems, and we have for almost 50,000 years without any heart disease, stroke, or cancer. But these days, conventional meat from your supermarket or butcher, especially beef, contains at least 39 pesticides, 12 antibiotics, three hormones, artificial food dyes, and many other toxic chemicals too numerous to mention, and so does conventional milk; it comes from the same place. Sorry, but pork is just as bad and often worse. Grass-eating animals have omega-3 fatty acids, which we all need.

In fact this is the real reason to eat meat at all. Omega-3 fatty acids are the building blocks of our nervous system, along with minor amounts of omega-6 and omega-9, and other fatty acids and amino acids. Cows and most other hoofed animals are genetically designed to eat grass. That's how they get these essential fatty acids into their muscle. Corn fed, farm-raised cows do not eat grass. They are fed corn and other processed grains to make them fat, just like you will get fat when you eat processed grains. This means that conventional cows do not have the essential fatty acids you need to be healthy, which is the only reason to eat meat anyway. Do not eat conventionally raised beef, or anything else that comes from an American farm cow. Eat only wild game or organically raised meat about once a week or less. There are lots of sources; check the internet or local farmers' markets.

I'm sorry, and I apologize to all you vegetarians. I totally respect your decisions not to eat meat for humane reasons, political reasons, environmental reasons, humanitarian reasons, or religious reasons. I support many of those reasons 100%. However, there is no good **nutritional argument** against eating healthy, organically raised meat or wild game on rare occasions. I could never condone eating meat or dairy products from a farm-raised cow or other conventional farm animal. I know vegetarians are healthier than the average person, but that's because they eat more vegetables and because the average American is more toxic in comparison. Vegetarians usually have a more health-conscious attitude in general. That's the only reason some of them look and feel so much healthier than the average American. But they could be even healthier. Not eating any meat, fish, dairy, poultry, or eggs will definitely create a deficiency of essential fatty acids, which means you will have to carefully supplement your diet if you want to be optimally healthy. You must have an intake of omega-3 essential fatty acids daily, or you cannot be optimally healthy, period! After all, these are the building blocks of your brain tissue and nervous system tissue, which by now I hope you feel is a rather important part of your body. The best source of omega-3-EFA's comes from fish and fish oil; but remember that the ocean is polluted so you can only have fish once or twice a week, due to the heavy metal toxicity. Everyone would benefit from fish oil supplements, but vegetarians especially need to supplement omega-3 fatty acids daily, or they cannot not be 100% healthy. And now you can get fish oil that is molecularly distilled to remove all the toxins, leaving only pure oil. Read your labels for the word "molecularly distilled" on your supplement label. Also, don't be fooled by the flax-seed oils and other vegetable oils. Yes, they are healthy and contain some essential fatty acids, but you would have to consume ridiculously large quantities in order to get the amounts you need on a daily basis. Chugging down an entire bottle a day of flax oil is just not practical.

Of course vegetarians always argue the point about meat, but they are wrong. No one wants to be wrong so they argue very strongly, but they are still wrong. Every study I have ever seen indicates the human digestive system is designed to process meat. Good, clean wild game, without any drugs, was one of the basic staples for many people of many cultures throughout the world, none of whom showed any signs of degenerative diseases. Only in the past 500-1,000 years since man has tampered with Mother Nature, has our food supply become tainted, and thus our bodies as well. But you should blame the government and the chemical and pharmaceutical companies, not the animals.

Vegetables and fruits should be at least 70% of each meal you eat, and about 50% - 60% of your total calorie intake. Most people are fiber deficient. This is actually one of the causes of health problems. You need to eat more fiber daily. You will get more fiber if you eat more vegetables. The rest of your diet should consist of fruit, nuts, seeds, and occasional clean, lean, meat or fish. Eat most of your food raw whenever possible. Steam some vegetables if you have to, but try not to boil or fry.

Why?

Boiling removes 80% of the nutrients and destroys the enzymes, which you then throw away in the boiled water. Frying is worse, by adding oxidized fats which are deadly toxins. Some soups are o.k. but only if you retain all the broth and eat it; but always make your soup from scratch with fresh ingredients, never canned or packaged. Remember, heat deactivates the enzymes, so raw is better, but soup is healthy too. At least it's not toxic if you make it with mostly organic ingredients. It's not junk food or in any way bad for you, just not as nutrient packed as raw veggies.

Pretty much 99.9% of everything you eat should come from the list above. I'm not going to give you lots of recipes or measurements of food. Everyone has a different personal taste, and I believe you should experiment with different combinations as much as possible. Try everything at least once. If you're not in love with a certain food combination then figure out what you would add or leave out to make it better. There are countless combinations of food from the above list that you can combine to make a wide variety of appetizing meals. If you have a specific health concern related to diet, consult your chiropractor, or a natural nutritionist. Just beware. If they recommend calcium supplements or whole-wheat bread and cereals, run away, and find someone who has done the research and knows what is really healthy. I will list a few basic food recipes just to get you started.

However this is *very* important:

Pick and choose from the list above and eat what you like. Be creative. Prepare your meals with love. Sit and eat with family or company. Don't watch TV or do anything else when you are eating. Concentrate on the food. Eat deliberately. Savor every bite. Chew all your food well. Digestion starts in the mouth. Appreciate your food. Appreciate your body. Appreciate health. Eat slowly and stop as soon as you feel satisfied. Don't wait until you are stuffed full, or until your plate is clean, as your indicator to stop eating. Eat to live, don't live to eat. As much as I love my family and as much as I appreciate the old family dinner traditions, it's not about the food, it's about your health.

These important steps can make a difference in your health almost as much as the actual ingredients you are eating.

Basic salad:

Make a list of every vegetable that you can think of that you would not mind eating. It should be a long list with lots of variety. Don't forget to include sprouts. Then pick at least seven to ten (you could use them all) vegetables to make your salad. You can make enough for two to three days, depending on what vegetables you pick and how fresh you buy them. Put them into separate sealed containers and keep them in the refrigerator. They will stay fresh if you squeeze a little fresh lemon juice on them. You should eat at least two of these salads every day. In fact they should be the biggest part of at least two of the four meals you eat each day. When you finish them in a day or two, go back to your list and pick a new combination of seven to ten; the variety of combinations will never end and will never let it get boring for you.

Salad dressing:
Extra virgin organic olive oil
Flax seed oil
Fresh squeezed organic lemon juice
Organic apple cider vinegar (optional)
Fresh and dried seasonings to taste

Breakfast:
Organic whole oats
Raw unprocessed local honey
Two pieces of fresh fruit
Or:

Mixed bowl of fresh fruit

A fresh fruit smoothie, or a fresh mixed vegetable juice drink, juiced fresh, just prior to drinking

Or:

Two to three organic eggs, soft boiled or poached (or raw)

Fresh fruit

Or:

My own cereal mix:

Almonds, sunflower seeds, pumpkin seeds, walnuts, flax seeds, raisins, sliced banana, and organic oat milk. (Or almond milk, or hazelnut milk)

Mix the dry ingredients together in a large sealed container. Each morning you can put as much as you want into a bowl, add the banana and your favorite nut milk. Instant breakfast in less than a minute! You can also add any berries to this if you like fruit on your cereal, or eat the fruit separately. Limit to one bowl a day, as this is very nutrient rich and calorie rich. This is a modified recipe I partially stole from Dr. James, and it's great. Again, try a different combination of nuts and seeds that are your favorites if you don't like mine.

Lunch:

Eat anything you want from the good food list, in any combination. Eat what you like (but no grains, dairy, sugar, or junk food). Lunch should be the biggest meal of the day, most days. Always have a salad whenever you can.

Dinner:

Eat anything you want from the good food list in any combination.

See, it's not that hard, and it's not that restrictive. I bet you will end up eating a bigger variety of meals now than you were before. Just remember: Every dinner does not have to include some animal protein. Eating meat and or fish one to two times per week is plenty. You can have great and filling vegetarian meals, with some different and exotic fruit combos for dessert.

Drink water. This is the most overlooked nutrient on the planet. Your body is made up of water more than anything else (except energy and space). There is water in every cell of your body, even your bone cells. You should be drinking so much water that there really is no room to drink anything else. Think back again to your ancestors. What was available to drink 50,000 years ago, coffee? No, just water. What was there to drink 40,000 years ago, juice? No, just water. What was there to drink 30,000 years ago, mochaccino-frappaccino? No, just water. What was there to drink 20,000 years ago, beer? No, just water. There simply is no reason to drink anything else, ever. This is a genetic requirement for health. Are you drinking enough water?

O.K., so we all know water is important, but do you know these statistics?

75% of your body is made of water.

75% of the earth is made of water.

75% of almost every living thing is made of water.

75% of all Americans are chronically dehydrated. (This applies to about half of the rest of the world population as well.)

For 37% of Americans, the thirst mechanism is weak and is usually mistaken for hunger.

One glass of water shut down night-time hunger pangs for almost 100% of dieters, in a University of Washington Study.

Even just mild dehydration will slow down your metabolism by at least 3%.

Lack of water has been found to be the #1 trigger of daytime fatigue.

Research shows that drinking 64 ounces of water a day can reduce joint pain, including back pain, for almost 80% of all pain sufferers.

Drinking more water and eliminating drinks that contain calories *significantly* aids in losing weight if you're on a diet.

A 2% drop in body water triggers nervous system dysfunction, including poor memory, trouble with basic math, difficulty focusing eyes for reading, and decreased computer skills.

Cancer research shows that drinking 64 ounces of water daily decreases the risk of colon cancer by 45%, breast cancer by 79% and bladder cancer by 50%.

Fluoride in drinking water is actually very unhealthy and can be toxic.

Most tap water is acidic compared to your body's pH (acid/base balance), which should be between 7.4 to 7.5. This is very important for healthy cellular function. Drinking acidic tap water is very stressful to your body and decreases your health. Test it. If it is acidic, fix it! You can fix it by adding a tiny pinch of baking soda and a few drops of fresh lemon.

The formula to figure out how much water is right for you is this:

You need an ounce of water for every two pounds of body weight, every 24 hours. So if you weigh 150 pounds, you need to drink at least 75 ounces of water every 24 hours. Got it? Body weight in pounds, divided by two, equals the number of ounces. Remember this is not from when you wake up until suppertime. This is from 12 noon until 12 noon the next day, so it's not as hard as you think. Get a 20-ounce bottle and fill it with water at least three times each waking day. That will be 60 ounces today and another 20 tomorrow morning, that's 80 ounces already. Drink your water slowly all day long, preferably at room temperature so as not to stress your body's internal temperature regulation. Try not to drink too much water during mealtime. You don't want to dilute the digestive fluids in your stomach too much. In fact it would be best not to drink anything at all during the meal. Drink more water before and after meals and little to none while actually eating.

Here is the list of foods you should <u>never</u> eat, and why:

Don't eat a lot of fungus or yeast-containing foods, like beer, wine, bread, especially fresh, warm bread, and some mushrooms. Why?

These foods can promote fungal and yeast growth in your body, which in turn may compete with the beneficial organisms needed for digestion and production of B-vitamins. There are beneficial microorganisms living in your body that you need for survival and health. Many different bacteria in your intestine and colon for example, aid in digestion, produce vitamins, and compete with other unhealthy microbes to keep them at bay. This is the main reason you get digestive problems and other bowel problems when you take an antibiotic prescription. The drug kills the good bacteria as well as the bad bacteria, leaving you depleted. These beneficial bacteria feed mostly on the fiber in your diet, which is another good reason to increase your fiber intake.

Why limit mushrooms?

Mushrooms grown in America are totally dependent on what they are grown on, which on American farms is usually dead, decaying matter from the already unhealthy and sick animals on the farm, or on plastic racks suspended in the air, which can render the mushrooms void of any real nutritional value. Once again here, if you want to eat mushrooms, eat only organically grown or certain imported mushrooms from another country. Some mushrooms do contain specific polysaccharides that appear to stimulate your immune system and may have other medicinal properties according to some research in Chinese medicine. These include shiitake, maitake, reishi, cordyceps, and turkey tail. Shiitake mushrooms contain *eritadenine*, a substance shown to reduce cholesterol levels. Maitake mushrooms contain a substance that has been shown to improve the symptoms of diabetes. Reishi mushrooms have been shown to have antioxidant and anti-inflammatory capabilities in some human studies done in 2004. Cordyceps have been shown to defend against Alzheimer's disease and increase endurance and exercise capacity in some Korean University studies. Turkey tail mushrooms have two polysaccharides that help restore immune function, according to Doctor Sarah Cimperman, a naturopath who treats cancer patients. My advice is to stick to only the types of mushroom mentioned here, preferably organic or imported brands only.

Most legumes should be avoided, except for lentils.

Why?

Most legumes contain aflatoxins, which are byproducts produced by a toxic mold on the bean. The chemical formula is $C_{17}H_{12}O_6$ if you want to go look it up. This is a very real problem. It is very difficult to kill this mold except by very high heat of cooking. If not cooked well, this mold and its byproducts have been shown to cause brain damage. The problem is that cooking for a long time over high heat destroys most of the nutritional value of the legume along with killing the mold. They won't make you sick if you cook them a lot, but they won't make you that healthy either, because the cooking process has now reduced their nutritional value by at least 85%. So they become sort of a "neutral" food. Also, very few people cook their peanuts and their peanut butter. Remember, peanuts are legumes, not nuts. Peanuts cause more allergic reactions and side effects than any other food allergy. Please avoid peanuts, beans, and peas that are commercially processed. Buy them raw and cook them well if you must eat them, but better to avoid them all together.

All conventional, grain-fed, farm-raised meat must be avoided. Like we said, cows should eat grass. Grain-fed (corn-fed) meat is directly linked to many chronic degenerative diseases, another one of those indisputable facts that no one can argue and that you can look up. The best steak houses boast that their steak is100% corn-fed beef. (100% heart-attack food) Order the wild fish and a salad instead. The only reason to eat meat is to get the EFA's, remember, and conventional meat has none because of the commercial grain-based diet they are fed. What conventional meat does have instead are pesticides, hormones, antibiotics, preservatives, and heavy metal toxic poisons. Please read *Diet for a New America* by Robbins; almost the whole book is about this subject and includes documentation from reliable sources. You should especially avoid deli meats, luncheon meats, and smoked meats. They contain the highest level of chemicals, including toxic dyes, nitrates, nitrites, and other poisons too numerous to mention. It's pretty simple: Don't eat or drink anything that comes from an American farm-raised cow! Someday Big Farmers may wise up and clean up their act, but don't count on it too soon.

Yes, this includes dairy products, and anything made with cow's milk. Why?

Same reasons stated above, only worse! Milk from conventional American farm cows is just about the most unholy of all the foods regarded as healthy. Everyone knows that Twinkies and fries and soda are bad for your health, but milk is actually labeled as a "health food." That is what makes it so dangerous. This is one of the items that most people consume to try to improve their health. Another good book to read on this subject is *Milk, The Deadly Poison*, by Robert Cohen, a respected industry researcher. In the book he reveals the many deadly toxic contents of your average milk carton. The large number of pesticides, as many as 39 different pesticides in some cases, are enough to make you want to avoid milk. But there are also about 12 antibiotics, many heavy metal toxins, at least three dangerous hormones, allergic proteins, viruses, bacteria, formaldehyde, which is a known carcinogen, and other deadly contents. Of all the toxic contents, the artificial bovine growth hormone may actually be the most dangerous. Artificial recombinant bovine growth hormone, r-BGH, is not only proven to be detrimental for human consumption by every report ever made on the topic, but it is a very controversial and hush-hush subject in the government and in the pharmaceutical industry.

Yes, the drug and chemical companies are involved in dairy farming too. They make the pesticides, antibiotics, and hormones that go into the cows. Monsanto Chemical and Pharmaceutical Company should be considered the biggest contributors to sickness and disease of human beings on the planet, simply because they are. The drugs and chemicals they make and sell to the farming industry alone are a multi-trillion dollar business. And they are a big reason why America is sick. Billions of those dollars have gone to influence the FDA and the U.S. Government to look the other way and even purposefully mislead the public on the dangers of consuming milk, according to Robert Cohen, Brian Vigorita, and Jane Heimlich, a nutritionist, author, and researcher. Many others agree, and many other books have been written on this subject.

These are strong words, but they are not opinions, they are facts. Even former Monsanto researchers like Robert Collier have come out and told the truth about the secret experiments that Monsanto did, proving that r-BGH is unhealthy and dangerous. They have the results of these experiments but will not publish them to the general public. In a lawsuit against them they claimed they did not have to release the results, citing trade-protection laws, and also stating that *"Monsanto will be irreparably harmed if such data is revealed."* During the trial hearing, Judge William H. Walls stated that **"The defendants have demonstrated the likelihood of competitive substantial harm if the information was released... and the court finds that the study's raw data is exempt..."** Only the government and the FDA know the full results. But so do the actual scientists who worked on the chemicals, and they are coming out and speaking against it. More than one expert who worked on the r-BGH says that the results show that EVERY animal tested in EVERY laboratory study got cancer and died from the artificial hormone!

This is just one of many cover-ups. For example, guess what happens to the many cows that die from all the chemicals injected into them? They get sold to the feed company who grinds them up, disease and all, and feeds them back to the surviving cows! This is according to experts like Howard Lyman, a cattleman who appeared on "Oprah Winfrey," stating that *"even cows with mad cow disease are sold to feed companies that grind them up into feed for other animals, including cows."* I couldn't make this stuff up. Get the transcripts from the Oprah show, or read one of the many books on the subject.

Judge Walls was correct. If the study results were released, who would ever drink milk again? Milk contains chemicals that caused cancer in every laboratory animal ever tested! That chemical is now in our milk supply. It is in your milk carton in your refrigerator right now. It is in every dairy product we consume. These are the people who should be appearing the most on Oprah, and on TV news shows, but they fear the wrath of the drug companies too much to let the truth be told. Imagine if you're a TV station and your main advertiser threatened to pull all its ads and close its accounts. That could be a half a million dollars per commercial every 15 to 30 minutes, 24 hours a day 365 days a year. That's over $876,000,000.00 (almost a billion) a year loss of revenue for the TV station.

How about some common sense? IGF-I is the most powerful growth hormone in humans. It has the same effect as r-BGH does in a baby calf. Do you think these hormones work to produce an effect? Of course they do; they're so powerful they accelerate processes that turn babies into adults. Once becoming an adult, the cow does not drink milk anymore. No animal on planet earth drinks milk or eats milk products as an adult, EXCEPT HUMANS, and we don't even have sense enough to drink human milk, we drink cow's milk! Why? (Why not monkey milk, dog milk, or rat milk? What's the difference?) Who decided it should be cows? Cow's milk is nothing like human milk. It's mostly indigestible. If someone offered you a pill containing a dose of IGF-I, the most powerful growth hormone in the human body, would you take it? I hope not. But every time you drink a glass of milk this is exactly what you are doing. Only you are taking a dose of a chemically engineered r-BGH made for baby cows, which has the same metabolic effect, and a dozen other side-effects, and kills every animal it is tested on.

Do you think there is no conspiracy? After the FDA privately reviewed all the findings, they published their approval article about it for the first time anywhere on Friday, August 24th, 1990. But two days earlier, on August 22nd, the *Journal of the American Medical Association (JAMA)* had jumped the gun and published their endorsement of the FDA's conclusion in the article, an article that no one had seen yet, including them! JAMA is supposed to be representative of America's doctors and is respected for unbiased review of medical issues. That is, unless Monsanto pays them millions of dollars to print what they want printed. Any article submitted to *JAMA* for review requires at least one week lead time for the article to appear. This is standard for most magazine publications. They printed their review and approval of the FDA findings before the FDA was done reviewing it to get any findings! Neat trick!

Back to common sense. If you're still in doubt, just do this experiment; *completely eliminate* all milk and dairy products from your diet, and anything else that comes from a conventional farm cow, for 100 days. Then, start eating them again noting carefully how you feel for about the next week or so, and then eliminate them again. If that does not convince you then nothing I say here will. But I will say it again anyway: Don't drink milk. If someone says differently, don't forget to ask them "Where did you read that...and can I . . .," oh, you know!

"Hey Doctor Bill, what about calcium?"

Well I already have another book to write, after that I will write a third book, just about calcium. This can be a long and very controversial subject too. I will try to keep it short and sweet here. FORGET ABOUT THE CALCIUM! The completely arbitrarily made up RDA for calcium in this country is 1500 mg per day. Our calcium intake in the U.S.A. is higher than in almost any other country in the world. Yet we have the highest rate of osteoporosis, broken hips, and rotten teeth than any other country. In countries like Africa, where there is little or no milk consumption and an average calcium intake of less than 400 mg per day, they have stronger bones and teeth, and no osteoporosis, another undeniable fact that you can go look up. But is anybody asking WHY?

Of course not, because if someone asks why, then you would have to give them the answer, and we wouldn't want that. No one should care how much calcium goes in your mouth or how much is circulating in your blood. It doesn't matter. What matters is how much calcium is being absorbed by your bones (and muscles and other places where it is needed). So the real question is; what causes bones to absorb more calcium? NOT more consumption, that's for sure. We are about to bust another big myth about health that nobody wants you to know, yet is an undeniable scientific fact that no one can argue. You actually already know the answer but you don't realize it yet. What causes a bone to absorb calcium? What causes a cell in your body to do anything that it does? *The signal it gets from the environment!* Here is how it works:

When a bone is stressed by a muscle contraction, that "stress", that pulling on the bone, becomes the environmental signal to absorb more calcium and other minerals to make the bone stronger and so support the stress of the muscle action. The chemical pathway that depends on the bone matrix actually laying down more minerals relies on vitamin D, among other things, for the process to happen. In fact, even the *Journal of the American Medical Association* published articles on studies that suggested that vitamin D plays a more important role in bone health than calcium, according to Dr. Robert P. Heaney, M.D., of Creighton University Medical School, in 2007. It does not matter how much calcium you take in, you could take a bottle a day. It will not increase bone density one bit unless you stress the bone with exercise and have the vitamins present as catalysts to promote the process of absorption. That's it, period.

If you're a couch potato, and do not do any weight-bearing exercise, then you can sit on the couch all day and eat an entire bottle of calcium everyday and I promise that you will get osteoporosis. But if you do weight-bearing exercise regularly and get some sunshine on your skin (to make vitamin D), then I promise you will not get osteoporosis, even if you never take a calcium supplement. If you eat green leafy vegetables daily, you will be getting enough calcium in your diet. But again I don't care how much is in your diet, I care how much is in your bones, and so should you. Good bone health depends on exercise and good nutrition. Bone density depends just as much if not more on potassium, magnesium, copper, vitamin K, and protein than upon calcium. A recent study published in the *Archives of Internal Medicine* in June 2006 stated that vitamin K alone could reduce the risk of hip fracture by 80%. If your doctor or nutritionist tries to put you on calcium supplements, please give them my number and have them contact me so I can show him this basic, simple fact in every scientific textbook on nutrition ever written. I really can write a book about this subject, but I think you get the point. It is mostly just dairy industry/drug company hype in advertising to sell you their junk. Please don't fall for it. Instead of watching all the lies on the TV commercials, go for a walk. Your bones will be better off... Next...

Avoid eating processed soy products! Yes, I'm sorry, but soy products are not healthy and that's a fact, not an opinion.

Why?

Most soy products are GMO, or genetically modified, but they are not labeled GMO. They are supposed to be by the year 2009-2010. We'll see what fast ones they pull then. For now, we don't know what genetically modified food is doing to us yet, but if it was not available to eat 40,000 years ago, it's probably not healthy now. Soy also contains high levels of a hormone that can upset your own natural hormonal balance. Processed soy products have become popular as a replacement for dairy and claim to be healthy but are not. Processed soy is a little better than drinking cow's milk, that's for sure, but I don't want you to think it is a "health food." Recent research is finally giving soy the bad rap it deserves. Luckily this research on soy is not as hard to find as the research that gives milk a bad rap. Research shows that the soybean also contains an enzyme inhibitor that causes digestive problems. The soy phytates cause mineral deficiency if taken in large quantity. It can reduce zinc and iron absorption. There is a lot of research on this. One good source is a study done by HY Son, A. Nishikawa, T. Ikeda, T. Imazawa, S. Kimura, and M. Hirose: *"Lack of effect of soy isoflavone on thyroid hyperplasia... Japan."* J Cancer Res. 2001, 92:103-108.

There are more recent studies on soy listed in the back of the book, all coming to the same conclusion: Soy is not only unhealthy, it can be dangerous. Some fermented soy products can be nourishing, like Tempeh and Miso used in Japan, but you must be sure the source of the soy is not genetically modified. Once again, avoid American products and use only imported products. Also on a common sense note: Did you ever see a soybean? Did you know that it's green? Guess what color the liquid is when you squeeze or press a soybean to make soy milk? It's GREEN. Did you ever see green soy milk? How do you think they get it to become white? Chemical processing, like bleaching, makes soy milk white, because marketers don't think they could sell as much if it was green. Chemicals left over from the processing of soy are still in your carton of soy milk. Send a box of it out to your local lab to be tested. After you get the list of chemicals they found in the analysis, let me know if you still want to drink it.

You can eat good, clean, organic soybeans that have been fermented, but that's about it.

Do not eat processed grains, please, please, *please*. Grains (processed grains) like white rice, breads, pasta, cereals, and pretty much anything made from white flour or white rice is very unhealthy. These foods are off limits.

Why?

Because I want you to live longer, and without diabetes, that's why. Sorry, but processed grains, along with dairy, are the two staples of the average American diet, and the main reason America is rated 37th on the world health index and dropping fast. We have more heart disease, stroke, and cancer than any other country, and this is why. All breakfast cereal is a deadly poison and should be avoided at all costs. In fact, I agree with the statements that I've heard at some lectures that I have been to, that say Kellogg's and General Mills and Post Cereals will be the next big class action lawsuit in this country, going the way of the tobacco industry. They know what is in that cereal box. They know that it's in no way healthy. They know that it is the major cause of diabetes in this country. Yet they continue to make TV commercials that say high-fiber cereal is good for you. It's a lie, period. High-fiber cereal is slightly less deadly than low-fiber cereal, so it's better, but it's the same as adding fiber to your cigarettes, or to your arsenic. Every morning millions of American moms are sending their kids to school with bowls full of poison in their stomachs. Please don't have any boxes of cereal in your house. Please don't walk down the cereal isle at the supermarket. You and your family will live a longer, happier, healthier life, guaranteed.

Why?

The reason is that processed grains, rice flour, white flour, corn, wheat, are all carbohydrates. Sugar is a carbohydrate. Glucose is one of the simplest forms of sugar. It is the kind of sugar your body uses for energy. Your body makes this sugar from almost any carbohydrate. YOU DO NOT NEED ANY SUGAR IN YOUR DIET, EVER, BECAUSE YOUR BODY MAKES ITS OWN, IN THE EXACT RIGHT AMOUNT AT THE EXACT TIME IT NEEDS IT. When you eat the longer-chain carbohydrate in the form of the processed grains I listed, they are broken down into simple sugar or glucose. Sucrose, white table sugar, is also a carbohydrate. You know that this is very unhealthy for you, and is off limits if you have diabetes, right? Your body can only handle a tiny little bit of sugar at a time from the outside. The sucrose in the cereal box, or the corn syrup, or high fructose corn syrup that they use to sweeten the cereal is already way too much sugar for your body to handle at one time. Then the grain itself, the wheat or corn that was processed to make the crunchy part of the cereal, also breaks down into sugar. Even sugarless cereal is all sugar, because it is all processed grain that becomes sugar when digested. Your body is now way overloaded with sugar. Where does this extra sugar go? It gets stored in small amounts in your liver as glycogen, another form of more complex sugar, and the rest, most of it, gets stored as fat, bad fat like palmitic acid, the kind you see around your waist, hips and thighs. You know that eating the ice cream or the candy bar is bad for you because it is too much sugar for your body to handle at once. But eating a bowl of cereal is the same thing. Eating a slice of white bread is the same thing. Eating a serving of pasta made from white flour is the same thing as eating a serving of Ben and Jerry's Ice Cream.

You don't care because you're not fat? O.K., guess what else happens? You still get diabetes anyway. Or pancreatic cancer. Or heart disease. Or a whole host of other chronic degenerative diseases. You see, your pancreas makes insulin. Insulin is a hormone that has very many important functions in your body. One of them is to transport glucose in and out of your cells. Insulin is knocking on the door of your cell membrane begging to get in. But your cell resists answering the call, because it is loaded with sugar and insulin already. This is what *insulin resistance* is. Insulin becomes toxic to your cells, and your cells resist letting it in by blocking the door. The problem is that cell door is the same specific door that vitamin C uses to get in and out of the cell, so it is blocked too. Many essential compounds that your cells need to function normally use the same door to get in and out of the cell that insulin does. But the door is blocked because you ate cornflakes for breakfast. It remains blocked because you ate a sandwich with white bread for lunch. It remains blocked because you ate white-flour pasta or a white potato for supper. Or you ate pie, or cake, or cookies for dessert after supper. Of all the foods you need to eliminate from your diet to be healthy, dairy and processed grains are the most important to get rid of. Dairy and processed grains are the main things that are killing Americans. Remember, there are 940,000 deaths each year, just from heart disease alone. The number of deaths from diabetes is not far behind. Easily 90% of these deaths could be prevented if you follow the suggestions in this book.

Another problem with processed grains in the "gluten sensitivity." This is a real systemic autoimmune disorder that masquerades as many other medical conditions, making it difficult to diagnose. A very large portion of the population, approximately 30% of people tested, have gluten intolerance, but many do not know it. Gluten is the protein in wheat, barley, and rye. According to Shari Lieberman, Ph.D., CNS, FACN, it has been directly linked to conditions such as celiac disease, ADD, arthritis, irritable bowel syndrome, Crohn's disease, colitis, and eczema. Studies done at the University of Maryland confirm this. Gluten sensitivity can be expressed at many different levels. Not everyone has celiac disease, but three out of ten people test positive for gluten-sensitivity at high enough levels to cause a problem. Another great reason to avoid processed grains at all costs.

There are so many books and scientific references on the deadly dangers of the foods listed above that I could not list them all. Yet, still, this factual information is controversial to some people and still meets a great deal of resistance. Please don't resist this information. These last few pages could save your life, literally. In fact, I'm sure that if you stop giving your kids processed grains and follow the advice in this chapter, you can totally eliminate almost 90% of ADD/ADHD symptoms and get your kids off of Ritalin and other equally dangerous, poisonous chemicals they may be taking for their symptoms of hyperactivity. It will also be harder to become overweight, since grains and dairy products can be very calorie-dense, especially when compared to vegetables and fruit.

And now for the obvious...

Avoid eating "junk" food. There is a reason they call it that you know. Soda, salt, sugar, junk food, any processed food, etc... Why should you stop eating these even if you are not overweight? You should know the answers to this one by now, especially if you have seen the movie *Super Size Me*. If you haven't, please go rent it. Pay attention to the doctors' revelations and to the statistics at the end of the movie.

I'll just mention a few things about junk food that should be obvious and add a few "whys" for each. Let's talk about soda first. Soda is one of the most popular drinks in the world. We know the sugar story, so diabetes and rotten teeth should be enough reason not to drink any soda. But the phosphoric acid in soda takes calcium out of bones and causes osteoporosis, as well as contributing to rotting your teeth. That's right, I said it *causes* osteoporosis. I've got the research; show me yours. Colas are the worst offenders of all soft drinks, because they have the strongest acids and the lowest pH levels. Would you add strong, harmful acids to your water before you drink it? Avoid all colas at all costs, ESPECIALLY DIET SODA, which is even worse. Aspartame is a known neurotoxin, and is illegal in many countries. If you have to make the choice of eating sugar or eating known, deadly, poisonous, toxic chemicals like sugar substitutes, then choose the sugar. It's better to avoid any soda at all costs.

Salt causes high blood pressure. Even your medical doctor has probably told you to reduce your salt intake to help lower your blood pressure. Well, it also dehydrates you, stresses your kidneys, and adversely affects the pH buffer systems in your body. Unlike grains and dairy, salt in small amounts won't kill you, but large amounts should be avoided for many reasons, not just blood pressure.

The usual processed foods and junk foods you know about are obviously not healthy foods. They contain hundreds of toxic chemicals not found on the label that you don't know about. For example if you see "red dye" or "artificial cherry flavor" on the label, it seems like one bad ingredient. But did you know that there may be as many as 100 different chemicals that make a dye or an artificial flavor? One hundred different unpronounceable, toxic chemicals all in one fake flavor, just called "artificial flavor." Please read your labels. Don't consume food dyes, artificial flavors, sugar substitutes, artificial colors, gums, thickening agents, or packaged foods with words on the label that you can't pronounce. If it does not grow on or walk on the earth naturally, don't put it in your body. If it was not available to eat 10,000 years ago, don't put it in your body. We are genetically adapted to eat what was available to eat on earth 50, 40, 30, 20, and 10 thousand years ago, and we did just fine for that entire time. If you couldn't find it on earth back then, don't buy or consume it now. It's that simple.

See, nutrition is not that hard. Don't put anything in your shopping cart that you, or someone, could not grow or hunt. That is the way it was supposed to be. In fact, if it has a long list of ingredients on the label then just don't eat it, eat the label instead; at least it might have come from a tree. (no, really, don't)

This is all well-researched and documented information, so please just stop eating these poisons. To list every junk food out there would take the rest of the book. You know most of them. Obviously you should avoid all fast-food restaurants like McDonalds. They are among the worst combinations of foods that you could eat, but they also have added chemicals in most of their food that make you hungry and secretly make you crave more of their food. Sounds unbelievable but true. I strongly recommend you rent the movie *Super Size Me* and note what the experts say about fast food. Another good book called *Fast Food Nation* is also well worth reading.

One of the worst offenders in the fast-food chains is the trans-fats. Again, something you should know about. If not, it is well worth doing a little research on trans-fats and how deadly they are. They are also one of your biggest enemies against the battle of the bulge, as well as being so bad for your heart. According to Lisa Mosing, MS., RD., FADA, of *Lifescript Nutrition*, trans-fats are now directly linked to heart disease. In a national survey she states that almost 94% of people know about trans-fats danger, but only 73% were actually concerned about the health consequences. Please be concerned. Researchers at Wake Forest University in North Carolina monitored a group of monkeys who were fed the typical American diet of 35% calories from fat. But half ate a diet higher in trans-fats but the exact same amount of calories. The trans-fat group increased its weight by 7.2% or more, while the other group only increased 1.8%, despite the fact that both groups consumed the same number of total calories and grams of fat. All fats are not equal. The researchers also concluded that saturated fats (trans-fats) provide no nutritional value and only have harmful effects on your body, contributing to disease.

A final note here on a specific food that many people still eat; Doughnuts. Nutritionists will agree that the five worst foods you can eat are sugar, salt, white flour, milk and trans-fats. I pretty much agree with that. Well, commercial doughnuts have all five! Commercial doughnuts are made by deep frying them in oil that has been kept at high heat for a long time. The more you use the oil, and oxidize the oil, burning it into nothing but saturated trans-fat, the crispier the doughnuts. Guess where Dunkin Donuts and Krispy Kreme get their oil from? They buy the old, used oil from Burger King and McDonalds and other fast food chains. The same oil that was used for a week to fry your onion rings, fries, fish, and apple pies. They are all fried in the same oil, and that oil is kept hot all day long every day, so it is just right for making doughnuts crispy. Completely oxidized, saturated, and deadly. This sounds disgusting and it is, but I have reliable resource articles that prove this is true. I could not get McDonalds or Krispy Kreme to comment on the subject at all. It looks like they have something to hide. Please do not eat doughnuts. If you must on rare occasions, then go to your local bakery where they are fresh, and ask only for the doughnuts that are baked, not fried; but remember, they still contain four of the five most unhealthy ingredients you can eat. Try to avoid them as much as possible.

Here is some general advice on eating.

Breakfast should be a small- to medium-sized meal for the average person. Try not to ever skip breakfast; even if it is just a small piece of fruit, it is better than nothing. Lunch should actually be your largest meal of the day. Supper should be smaller. Have small, healthy snacks in between if you are hungry. Try not to eat anything at all within two hours of bedtime. Sit down and eat your meal slowly and deliberately, without distractions and preferably with someone else there for company. You'll eat slower and usually eat less.

Eliminate other toxins in your environment as well, whenever you can. Things like smoking, alcohol, drugs, make-up, commercial cleaning products, Teflon and other non-stick pans, microwaves (outlawed in many countries), antiperspirant with aluminum, most makeup, hair dyes (very deadly), etc., are all toxic to you body; and all cause negative effects, and must be dealt with by the stress response, which of course you have memorized by now or you wouldn't be reading this far yet, right?

Microwave ovens have been outlawed in some countries because of the real dangers they pose in your kitchen as an appliance, and because of what they do to your food to render it unhealthy. Why would you want a nuclear reactor in your kitchen anyway? Get rid of it.

Teflon pans contain perfluorooctanoic acid (PFOA), a chemical directly linked to cancer and birth defects. A law has been passed to ban it from use in most cooking utensils... a ban that takes effect in 2015!!! Why the long wait if they know it's so dangerous? Write and ask your friendly local neighborhood FDA representative, and your congressman and your senator, and PLEASE ask them why? (Remember, it's all about the money.)

A word about *"organic"*:

You may find going totally organic difficult, depending upon where you live, and also on your budget. As far as the cost goes, the more we buy organic and support organic farming, the lower the price will get. And there are some conventional foods that are less offensive than others. You can get by on some of these foods if nothing else is available organically.

The most contaminated foods are:

Peaches, nectarines, strawberries, white potatoes, raspberries, pears, apples, cherries, grapes, spinach, celery, and bell peppers. These foods contain the most toxic chemicals in the highest quantities and must be purchased as organic whenever possible, or avoided. Memorize this list. Peaches are the most contaminated fruit, followed by strawberries. Celery is the most contaminated vegetable, at least at the time of writing this book.

The *least* contaminated foods are:

Sweet corn, avocado, cauliflower, asparagus, onions, peas, broccoli, and garlic. If you cannot find or afford the organically grown version of these foods, you could get by using the conventionally grown, especially avocados, which are the least contaminated of most conventionally grown foods. Just keep in mind that whenever you can, buy organic produce.

Whichever you choose, please do not forget to wash all your produce very carefully, even the organic food. The problem is, even though they are grown naturally with no chemicals, once picked and put on the truck, they are sometimes sprayed with pesticides. How could this be? Well, the government has a strict code for organic farming. The soil is tested and must be chemical free. So the food is perfectly clean when it is picked. But the government does not have the same restrictive code for the trucking industry, so they can do whatever they want. Some organic farmers are now making deals with the trucking industry to have them spray their produce after it leaves the farm. This protects the produce during travel and gives it more shelf life in the supermarket. Anything for a little more profit, right? The inside of the produce is still 1000% better than conventionally grown food, which has the nasty chemicals inside and out. But the skin of much organic produce is coated with poison. So wash all your organic produce thoroughly, even the ones you peel, like oranges.

O.K., let's briefly mention supplements.

I used to fall into the trap of taking a large amount of supplements. Every time I went to the heath-food store there was something new to try. The sales pitch was always that the food supply no longer has the vitamins and minerals we need because farming has depleted the soil. This is only partially true. Remember what I said in the very beginning of the book about everyone having an agenda, a product to sell? Well, there's no difference here. People lived for almost 50,000 years without supplements and did not have chronic degenerative diseases. Some farm soil may be depleted, that's true, and it is also polluted with commercial fertilizer that contains a lot of heavy metal toxic poisons. So we are now only going to eat lots *organic* fruits and vegetables whenever possible. They have plenty of vitamins and minerals if you eat enough of them. They did not deplete the soil enough to cause disease for the first 40,000 years that they grew on earth. Plus, organic farmers use organic fertilizers, which replace nutrients into the soil. Since we are now going to make vegetables and fruit the major part of our diet from now on, we should be getting more vitamins and minerals than ever before. Since I added more fresh food and decreased my supplements, I feel great. And so do my patients that I advise to do the same.

Keeping this in mind, you should be able to keep your supplements to a minimum if you adjust your diet to the good foods described previously in the "good food" section of this chapter. There are some things that you do need to supplement, however.

Remember that there is little or no omega-3 fatty acids left in our food supply, except in cold-water ocean fish, but they all contain mercury and other pollutants. So we all need to supplement with omega-3 essential fatty acids. This is especially true if you are a vegetarian, but everyone is deficient. Make sure you get a source of fish oil supplement that is molecularly distilled to remove all the toxins, leaving only pure fish oil. Read your label carefully. Use this supplement daily forever.

If you need more convincing, or want to learn more about our contaminated food supply, please get a copy of *Fateful Harvest* by Duff Wilson. This is a <u>must read</u> for everyone if you plan on eating any food at any time in the near future, or for the rest of your life. Read it very carefully; you will be amazed.

Back to supplements. I also find that most everyone is deficient in the mineral magnesium, partially because of diet, but mostly because of the overload of calcium we have been tricked into consuming. We simply take in too much calcium. This causes a deficiency in magnesium because these two minerals are needed in almost equal amounts. For example, calcium is needed to make muscles contract. An equal amount of magnesium is needed to make those same muscles relax. When there is too much calcium and not enough magnesium, then your body starts to draw magnesium out of your bones and organs to try and make up the difference, creating a deficiency. Both magnesium and calcium are needed in many places in your body, not just bones and muscles. It is the overload of calcium in our diet that is creating our magnesium deficiency. Calcium is put into everything because of the osteoporosis hoax we talked about earlier. It is in your orange juice; it is "fortified" in almost every processed food you eat. Big business, bad health. Everyone needs to supplement with magnesium to make up the difference. Be sure when going to your health food store that you get plain magnesium with no calcium in it. They will want to sell them to you together, but don't fall for it, especially since the calcium content will always be greater than the magnesium content, adding to the problem. Don't forget to check your multivitamins, too. If they have high calcium content… more than 400 mg… then switch to another brand.

A good, all natural, organic, vegetarian source of a multivitamin is also good to have around. But don't take them every day. Eat good food instead. Take the multivitamin once or twice a week or when you have slipped and are not eating well. That's about it, EFA's, Magnesium, and an occasional Mult-vitamin. That's all the supplements I recommend on a regular basis for everyone, although a few others should be mentioned here and kept on hand by many people.

It is a good idea to have some vitamin C on hand to take once in a while too, especially in the winter, or if you have been eating any sugar, or if you have been stressed, or not sleeping well. Vitamin C is used by every single one of the fifty trillion cells in your body. During times of stress or healing, it is used up even faster. If you are sick, stressed, or healing from an injury, then take vitamin C two to three times a day until you are back on track. Take between 1000 and 2000 milligrams during those times.

In the wintertime, if it is cold where you live and you are not getting out in the sun very much, then it would wise be to supplement with some vitamin D. It is a necessary catalyst for many processes in your body, not just building strong bones. Don't take vitamin D in a high dose, or daily throughout the year. Vitamin D is a fat soluble vitamin that is easily stored in your body and can be toxic in very large amounts. The less sun exposure, the more vitamin D supplement you may need; the more sun exposure, then the fewer vitamin D supplements you'll need. Just go outside on a sunny day.

Other supplements may be beneficial for helping with certain conditions, but remember, find the cause of your condition and get rid of that so you will not need the supplement. Don't try to "treat" your condition yourself by using a ton of supplements. That's outside-in; that's practicing medicine. Consult an expert if you have a specific condition, or if you think you have a deficiency. Or just follow all of the advice in this book and you won't have a deficiency.

A few other good things to have around that can boost your health are probiotics, and locally made raw unprocessed honey. These will help boost your immune system. Honey is a complete food, and has antiviral and antibacterial effects. It also has plenty of vitamins and minerals, but not in the supermarket brand of honey. Processing just turns it into fancy sugar. Be sure to get your honey raw and unprocessed, and if you have allergies, get it made locally to help you with your allergies. It is available in many local health food stores, although it would be even better to find a beekeeper and buy it directly from the source.

Probiotics are the beneficial bacteria in your body that we mentioned before. The natural flora of microorganisms in your digestive system is essential for good health, but they are very delicate. For example, if you have taken an antibiotic for an infection, the drug kills the good as well as the bad bacteria. (A very overused drug that should be avoided whenever possible.) You must replace the good bacteria as soon as possible. Taking a multiple probiotic is the best way. Keep a bottle in your refrigerator for emergencies; it will last a year if kept cool. Also remember that these bacteria feed on the fiber in you diet, so keep a good intake of natural fiber from raw food daily.

You don't need a stack of books on nutrition. If you want further information, get a simple college textbook used to teach nutrition courses. That is all you'll ever need. You certainly don't need a diet book. All you need is this chapter. Start eating the foods I recommend, and start eliminating the foods that are offensive to your health. Do it slowly, and gradually, without any stress. Start by adding the good foods. Don't start by denial. No negativity, no stress. Remember, getting rid of illness is done by adding more health. Don't use the word "diet." Like everything else, this is a lifestyle choice. Simply choose more health and less disease. Don't keep chasing darkness; just open the door and let more light in. Over time it will become easy, especially once you start experiencing the health benefits for yourself. Your goal is to add more health; it is never to *deprive* yourself, to *lose* anything like weight, or to associate with anything that is in any way *negative* or stressful, ever.

You say you don't want to do all this just be healthy? That's o.k., so long as you know that you will just be sick. Remember, taking away health allows more disease. You can't be a little pregnant, and you can't be a little healthy. You're either healthy or you're not. And "symptoms" are poor indicators of health. You only want to let a little bit of the light in and keep most of the darkness? That's alright; I have the secret formula to ensure chronic degenerative disease too. (With a double-your-money-back guarantee)

The secret formula for diabetes is:
Diabetes = Burgers, hot dogs, fries, soda, doughnuts, milk, sugar
The secret formula for high blood pressure is:
High B.P. = Burgers, hot dogs, fries, soda, doughnuts, milk, sugar
Cancer = Burgers, hot dogs, fries, soda, doughnuts, milk, sugar
ADHD = Burgers, hot dogs, fries, soda, doughnuts, milk, sugar
Stroke = Burgers, hot dogs, fries, soda, doughnuts, milk, sugar
Disease = Burgers, hot dogs, fries, soda, doughnuts, milk, sugar
To get most degenerative diseases you can think of:

Just apply the above formula.

Are you getting this? See, sickness and disease are not hard, either. In fact, it's easier than health and wellness. Just follow the above formula. It's your choice, but don't forget, you have to live (or die) with it.

"Tell me what you eat, and I will tell you what you are."
Anthemme Brillat Savarin

Let's end the chapter on a positive note. Here is a quote from an unknown source about the garden of your daily personal life.

For the garden of your own personal life, this is what you should plant:

Three rows of peas: Peas of mind, peas of heart, peas of soul.

Four rows of squash: Squash gossip, squash indifference, squash grumbling, squash selfishness.

Four rows of lettuce: Lettuce be faithful, lettuce be kind, lettuce be patient, lettuce love one another.

Three rows of turnips: Turnip for meetings, turnip for service, turnip to help a friend.

Four rows of Thyme: Thyme for each other, thyme for family, thyme for friends, thyme for health.

Water your garden freely with patience and love. There will be much fruit in your garden because you reap what you sow.

I include this here because your attitude towards food, like your attitude toward anything, is always the most important ingredient.

Chapter 8

...Give it a Rest...

"Work when there is work. Rest when you are tired. One thing done in peace will be better than ten things done in panic... You are not a hero if you deny rest; you are only tired."

Susan McHenry

It may seem silly to have an entire chapter telling you to go to sleep at night. But, since rest and sleep are required ingredients for your body in order to be healthy, it is definitely worth mentioning. Over the last 24 years of continued research, I have found that 50% of all Americans have significant trouble sleeping at night. And over those years I have seen that this problem is getting worse instead of better. This always amazes me, because sleeping seems like such a natural part of life. But when I started to have sleep problems myself many years ago, I decided to tackle this topic head-on. I learned a lot and I think it is important to share with you what I found, so please don't skip over this chapter; you may be surprised.

An interesting study was done at Boston University School of Medicine a few years ago on sleep. After an extensive review of thousands of clinical cases, one of the conclusions and statistics was that both sleeping too long and not sleeping long enough, can be very detrimental to your heath. In the study, both men and women who slept for 9 hours or longer were 70% more likely to die over a 14-year period than those who slept seven to eight hours. Those that slept for six hours or less had a 50% higher death rate.

Results from many sleep studies, including the famous *Framingham Heart Study*, now show that the optimum average nightly sleep-time should be between seven to eight hours. This time frame has been shown to be directly related to lowering your risk of heart disease.

Sleep time is when your body heals the most efficiently. There is actually a lot of physiology related to sleep. Hormonal changes take place. Your body temperature changes. Obviously your state of consciousness changes. Different parts of your nervous system are stimulated when you are sleeping compared to when you are awake. It is actually a complicated process and is just plain essential for good health. There are tons of studies on this subject. Lack of sleep is stressful and causes the stress response, which means losing too much sleep can cause all the same degenerative conditions as eating too much sugar or anything else that can elicit that "fight or flight" response that we have previously discussed.

So we have determined that sleep is important. Seven to eight hours of sleep is optimum. Six hours is the minimum, and nine is the maximum. Any more or less is actually unhealthy and will cause problems. These are the scientific facts. But how do we get to sleep if we are having trouble?

As it turns out, your body, especially your brain and nervous system, likes routines and schedules. The more you can schedule things and put everything into a daily routine, the better. This reduces stress in many ways. Everything you do that is routine and you don't have to think much about will take stress off of your body and your mind. In fact, you should eat your meals close to the same time every day. You should exercise at the same time every day. And most of all, you should go to sleep at the exact same time, and wake up at the exact same time, every day. This is very important. This is one of the most important ways to get a better night's sleep. It is also one of the best ways to reduce your stress and increase your health. You want to train your brain and nervous system to sleep and wake up at the exact same times to set your internal clock, also called your biological clock, or your circadian rhythm. This is a very real thing and important for health. You may have heard of circadian rhythm from, you guessed it, high school biology class. Your body functions depend on these rhythms. Actually, all of life depends upon these rhythms or cycles, which coincide with the cycles of the earth's rotation and orbit, with the moon and the tides.

Please don't think this is abstract; it's not. This is science. It is based on the 24 hours of the day, divided into three equal parts or time periods. Within these three 8-hour time periods there are actually two subdivisions, making a total of six 4-hour periods of time in a single 24-hour cycle. Two of these 4-hour time periods should be spent sleeping. And it is very important to make sure that it is the same eight hours every twenty four hours. Ideally this should be from 10:00 at night until 6:00 in the morning. For optimal health you should stick as close to these times as is reasonably possible. You can adjust these times up to approximately 30 minutes either way and still get by, but the most important thing is, once you find your most convenient bedtime and wake time, stick to it exactly to the minute, and never change it. This means if you have to get up for work at 5:45 a.m. then you must go to bed no earlier than 9:45 p.m., and no later that 10:45 p.m., seven days a week. This means that even if you don't have to wake up early for work on Saturday or Sunday, you still should go to bed by 10:45 and wake up at 5:45. Sorry, but that's the way it works for optimal health. This is your sleep time. It's yours. You own it, forever.

However, don't despair. The trick is the morning wake up time. That is what will eventually set your internal clock. Once you start waking up at 6:00 without an alarm clock, feeling rested and refreshed, then you know your clock is working right, and your biorhythm is in "sync." Let the alarm clock ring everyday at that exact same time, forever. But, if you stay up a little later on Friday or Saturday night once in a while, that's o.k. Go to bed whenever, but still let that alarm ring at 6:00 a.m. That will never change. Then, if you have the time, you can go back to bed again to catch a few more winks. Make sure that you are awake first. Don't keep your alarm clock within arm's reach of your bed. Be sure you have to move your body to shut it off. Then go back to bed if you want. Your internal clock won't be too upset if you do it this way, once in a while.

Another thing about alarm clocks. Since you are going to wake up to it every day, seven days a week for the rest of your life, make it pleasant. Kill the buzzer. Get a clock radio and set your clock alarm to music. Pick your favorite music station, or set it up to a favorite tape or CD, something gentle and relaxing. No one wants to be startled by a harsh noise first thing in the morning. That would be stressful, like someone sneaking up behind you and scaring you, causing the stress response. Remember, no stress, especially to start your day. Think of how it was 20,000 years ago. No clocks, no alarms, no deadlines to meet, or even a job to go to. Yet everyone woke up at about 6:00 in the morning, everywhere, all around the world. Their biological clocks were set at a very young age and never wavered. They woke up to the sound of singing birds, or babbling brooks, or by the light of the sun. And it was the same every day, seven days a week, for their entire lives. In fact, every day was the same day. There was no difference between Sunday and Wednesday. It was always just another day. Different days of the week are a manmade invention to help control society and to cause you more stress. There is no other reason to have them, is there? It just helps keep lives a little more organized.

There was an interesting survey done on cases of people who died of heart attacks. After reviewing thousands and thousands of cases over many years, it was found that most heart attacks occurred on, you guessed it... Mondays, by far! Guess what time on Mondays most people have heart attacks? Early AM - to mid-morning. This statistic is amazing. No other living animal on earth knows there is a difference between Monday and Tuesday, except humans. And we only invented the difference in our minds, about 6,000 years ago. Before that we didn't know there was a difference, either. And the heart attack statistic is not even close to being high on any other day compared to Monday. How could this be? There really is no difference between Monday and any other day, except in the minds of humans. Do you see how powerful your mind is? Do you see how attitude affects your health? The stress of the Monday morning deadline for work is killing people.

Let's move on to other sleeping tips. You should not do any strenuous exercise for approximately 90 minutes prior to bed time. You should not do any exercise at all, even light, easy exercise, within 20 minutes of bed time. The reason is that your heart rate increases during exercise, and it takes a long time to get your heart rate down to what is called "resting heart rate," which is necessary for proper sleep. Other physical and hormonal changes occur during exercise that can interfere with sleep also. Late night is the time to wind down and prepare your body and your mind for rest. For most people, exercise is best done in early morning, and for others it may be best in the late afternoon to early evening, but never right before bed. We will talk more about this in the chapter on exercise.

No late night snacks. For reasons similar to those stated above, you should never eat right before bedtime either, or, the worst habit of all, eating in bed. Eating requires digestion, and digestion requires a long list of specific physiologic functions in you body. Your stomach starts churning and contracting, blood flow to your digestive system and the rest of your body, changes dramatically. Chemical reactions are taking place to help process the food, and move it along the system, filter it, absorb what you need, and eliminate the rest. Even hormonal changes take place during digestion. It is a very active process, and definitely can upset sleep patterns. Since you are now going to be in bed at about ten o'clock almost every night, this translates into no eating large meals after 8:30 p.m., and no eating at all after 9:30 p.m.

Once you actually go to bed there are other things that you can do that will aid in sleeping and also aid in your quest for better health. For one, don't watch television as a sleep aide. This is a big mistake, although I have heard of some doctors actually recommending it. Ask them: Where did they read that and can you get a copy? Television is stimulation. Although there is very little, if any, intellectual stimulation from 99% of TV, it is still sound stimulation and light stimulation to your senses. It can still be "sensed" and therefore it makes your nervous system fire impulses. The room where you sleep should be as dark as possible. The room where you sleep should be as quiet as possible. These are very important factors for consistent quality sleep. Research proves that they are beneficial. Please go out of your way to make your bedroom as quiet and as dark as you possibly can, and be sure to use the bedroom for sleeping. Not for dining or entertainment.

And what about sleep positions; are they really important? For your health, please do not sleep flat on your stomach. You can pick any other sleep position you want, on your side, on your back, the fetal position, anything, but not on your stomach. This is not as related to falling asleep easier, as it is related to the health of your spine and nervous system. We discussed already how important it is to keep your spinal column in alignment. It is also very important to maintain the proper curvature in your spine that you are supposed to have from the side. Sleeping on your stomach can upset the natural curve of your spine. In fact I guarantee that it will. Lying face down causes your head to be turned to one side. Sleeping like that can change the shape of the disc in your spine, irritating nerves and causing a whole host of problems. Constant pressure on a joint changes the shape of the joint. This is not a theory but a fact used in dental practices on a daily basis. This is how braces work to change the position of your teeth. Teeth are always straight, but they may point in the wrong direction as they exit your gums, and so they appear crooked. They are as straight as a pencil, but pointing at the wrong angle. A dentist wraps a wire around your tooth, and pulls on it with constant pressure. This pressure is transferred to the joint in your jaw where the tooth originates. The constant pressure on the joint causes the joint to change shape over time, and the tooth slowly shifts to the better position. The dentist could make those teeth point in any direction he wants to, given enough time and pressure. This is no different than any other joint in your body, including the joints between your spinal bones. Sleeping on your stomach with your head turned for 7 to 8 hours every night will cause the disc in your spine to change shape too, just like the pressure of braces. You will eventually lose the natural shape of your neck, and this will predispose you to a lot of different problems, mostly stiff necks and headaches. I believe that this is one of the biggest causes of headaches that there is, and once I show people how to correct the natural curve of their neck, more than 98% of them never get a headache again, even long time migraine sufferers.

For similar reasons as above, you should not sleep with too big of a pillow. In fact, the smaller the pillow the better it is. The further away from the mattress your head gets the more pressure and distortion on your spine. Over time this will cause the same curvature problems that I just described for stomach sleeping, and the same long list of symptoms. If you learn to just stop sleeping on your stomach and use a small pillow from now on, then it was worth the price you paid for this book. Just these two things alone could make you healthier.

Another word about pillows in general. I am all for all-natural products, but not in this case. Get a small, firm, pillow made of foam. Not down, not feathers, not corn husks, not barley husks, not fiber filled, not sand, not water -filled, not anything else but a quality foam. These other pillows are just not consistent. They are a different shape every night, and wear out five times faster than a foam pillow. Every night your head is at a different angle and your spine has to constantly adapt. Every night you are sending different signals to your brain and nervous system. We want routine. We want consistency. We want stress-free; we want boring! Boring is healthy.

Another important tip is to get rid of anything that provides you with electric heat or dry heat during the night, especially if you have a back or neck problem already or an injury of any kind. Heated water beds, electric blankets, heating pads and any other electric heat is dangerous, in more ways than one. Not only are electrical fires common from these items, but they are unhealthy. Dry heat dehydrates your muscles and your entire body. Remember that every cell in your body needs and uses water for almost everything that it does. You need an ounce of water for every 2 pounds of body weight, right? Keeping this dry heat in contact with your body dehydrates your system three times faster than normal. Since you are not replenishing this water during the night, you wake up dehydrated, tight, stiff, and sore. It will take you many hours and a lot of water to get you back to normal. Also, constant heat for that log of a period of time will cause increased swelling and inflammation if you have an injury or suffer from arthritis or a number of other conditions. If your medical doctor or next door neighbor says anything different, tell them to call me. Therapeutic application of heat is usually moist heat, and it is designed to work over short time periods, from 10 to 20 minutes only, NOT 8 hours.

Finally, let's talk about what you sleep on for approximately one third of your entire life.

Because you spend so much time on it, you should take care to select a mattress of good quality and proper firmness. Firmness ratings of mattresses are based on how much weight they are able to support properly. They are not based on how good the mattress is for you. The most extra-firm mattress is not always the best for you. When you lie down on a mattress, you should be able to "sink in" slightly, to support the natural curves of your spine. Too firm of a mattress will flatten out your curve over time, and too soft of a mattress will let you sink in too much and force your spine into a bowl, or a "C" shape. A soft mattress is designed to support up to 150 pounds in a proper sleep position. If you weigh 150 pounds or less and sleep alone in your bed, then this is the correct firmness rating for you. An extra-firm mattress is designed to support in excess of 400 pounds, so if you weigh more than 400 pounds, or you and your spouse together total more than 400 pounds, then you may need the extra-firm mattress. However, if this is the case, you need to follow the advice in this book and get your body weight down to less than 400 pounds. Mid-range mattresses, above soft but below extra-firm, like medium to firm, are designed to support between 150 and 400 pounds, and this is the firmness that most people should seek. Of course mattress stores and salesmen will not tell you this information, because they want to sell you the firmest mattress possible. Extra firmness means more and better foam and more and better springs, which means more and better profits. My advice is to tear off the label on the mattress that says "do not tear off this label" and write to the mattress company directly, and they will tell you this information about mattress ratings. In general, don't buy a mattress through the mail; go to the store and lie down on it with your spouse or sleeping partner, and see how it feels. Make sure you sink in a little, but not too much.

Also, I advise against buying a "pillow mattress" or the kind of bed that is raised on one end. These mattresses cannot be flipped and turned, and this is essential for proper mattress wear. Most all mattresses contain foam, or springs, or a combination of both. Constant pressure on foam makes the foam wear out. The same goes for the springs in any mattress. It is important to have equal wear on the mattress so you have consistent support through the life of the mattress. This means that you must turn your mattress from head to toe, every month or so. Then the next month you should flip the mattress from bottom up. If you flip your mattress every other month, and in between, turn your mattress every other month, then it will wear out equally, and support you consistently over the life of the mattress. This will also extend the life of your mattress. But keep in mind that mattresses still wear out. At the most, even the best mattresses will only support you properly for about seven to ten years. Then they must be replaced. PLEASE do NOT hand down your mattress to your children or any other family member. After seven to ten years, throw it out.

The only exception to this is the new style mattresses that have an adjustable inflatable air bladder instead of foam or springs. These mattresses seem expensive, but last 20 years or more and only need the air bladder to be replaced once it starts to leak air. It costs twice as much as a regular bed, but can last three times as long, so they are worth investing in if they are within your budget.

If you review and combine all the information in this chapter, you will have mastered the basics for a good night's sleep. All the points are important, but consistency and routine are the keys. Develop a good bedtime and sleep routine, and keep your bedtime and sleep ritual exactly the same every night, and you will train yourself to sleep better eventually, and the consistent schedule and routine will reduce your stress, automatically making you healthier.

"May we all wake up laughing, and leave laughter in our wake."

Swami Beyondananda

CHAPTER 9

EXERCISE
The Final "Ingredient"

"When stressed, anxious, nervous, worried, mad, distraught, or in despair, go for a walk and observe nature..."

Anonymous

Remember in the chapter on stress when we determined that the "fight or flight" response happens every time your nervous system interprets an environmental signal as stressful? This response raises your heart rate, your cholesterol, your blood pressure, and your blood sugar. This was an appropriate response for our ancestors because it prepared them to run or fight, either of which would require them to "use up" the adaptive changes in physiology that your nervous system has provided for your body. This means that back then, a person would actually run, or fight, using his muscles hard, breathing faster, using that extra blood sugar, and that extra cholesterol. In today's society, the response is still the same, but we don't use our bodies properly to respond to the stress. We just go home and complain about it, watch TV, eat junk food, or all three, adding to stress's negative effects. The next time you feel stressed by your boss, co-worker, or spouse, go for a run! That is what you were supposed to do in the first place; exercise your body hard until you work up a sweat. Then you have appropriately "used up" some of your stress-response chemicals, and they will have much less of a negative effect on your body.

In his ground-breaking books, Dr. James L. Chestnut B.Ed, MSc., D.C., refers to exercise as a genetically required *"ingredient"* in the formula for health. I agree. For almost 50,000 years human beings worked very hard on a daily basis just to survive. Our bodies have adapted to this strenuous hard work over generations, and now exercise is a required part of any healthy lifestyle. Exercise aids in proper digestion. Exercise aids in proper sleep. Exercise aids in relieving pain. Exercise aids in a positive mental attitude due to the hormones, like serotonin, that are released. Exercise has been shown to aid in the recovery of almost every chronic degenerative disease in our society. *"Exercise induces the normal expression of the genome"* or your genes, according to F.W. Booth, Ph.D. In the *Journal of Applied Physiology*, F.W. Booth also states that physical inactivity is the third leading cause of death in the America and contributes significantly to the second leading cause of death, obesity, accounting for more than 10% of all deaths.

Here is another direct quote from Dr. Chestnut's book:

> *"Data clearly demonstrates that exercise induces transient increases in transcription of metabolic genes in human skeletal muscle. Moreover, the findings suggest that the cumulative effects of transient increases in transcription during recovery from consecutive bouts of exercise may represent the underlying kinetic basis for the cellular adaptations associated with exercise training."*
>
> **Pilegaard, et. al. "Transcription regulation of gene expression in human skeletal muscle during recovery from exercise."** *American Journal of Physiology Endocrinology Metabolism* 2000. 279 (4): E806-E814.

This research statement, and many others like it, proves that exercise positively affects gene expression. Therefore, it is a required ingredient for normal, healthy cells in order for them to stay normal and healthy.

Many exercise books state that the minimum amount of exercise required is 30 minutes a day, three days a week, with 20 of those 30 minutes being some type of aerobic exercise. Here I disagree. Our ancestors would typically hike out six miles or more, hunt and gather food, and then carry the gathered food, including heavy animal carcasses, at least six miles back to home. This was done on an almost daily basis, and that was just for food. In between they would construct shelters, carry water, cut and carry wood for fire, prepare all food by hand, and a lot of other physical activities. Then at the end of the day they would play with their children or dance around the fire. That was their *minimum* activity. Then occasionally they would climb mountains, cross deserts, and run away from predators. Does that all sound like 20 to 30 minutes a day, three days a week? We simply do not exercise enough in America. There is plenty of research that shows that our ancestors were in a similar physical condition as the average modern day Olympic athlete. There is plenty more research that America is one of the most overweight, out of shape, and overall unhealthy countries in the world. Think maybe you should take the stairs next time instead of the elevator? I'm sorry, couch potatoes, but you will never be healthy, no matter what else you do, if you do not perform some type of exercise on a regular basis.

There are many good books dedicated entirely to exercise. Unfortunately there are even more bad books dedicated entirely to exercise. Even some of the not-so-good "experts" on exercise who write these books have some beneficial basic information, but it really depends upon what you want out of your exercise routine. Why was the exercise book written in the first place? Well, the main reason is usually to make money off of an unsuspecting public. The other is to gain popularity so you will consider them an expert and buy their exercise equipment or join their gym, again, the bottom line being more money for them. If you're planning to run a marathon, then you need to exercise and train like a marathon runner. If you only want to lose weight, then your exercise routine may be different.

Some exercise theories are great for long distance runners, some others are better for professional athletes, some others are better for those who just want to lose weight. Some exercise routines are more suited for rehabilitation from injuries, and some are better for professional bodybuilders, and some are better for those who just want to shape up a little. Do you want to be a professional bodybuilder? Great, then go for it. But that is not the purpose of this book or this chapter. We are after improved health.

The latest craze now is more intense exercise but for much shorter periods of time. Anything that takes less time always sounds good to most Americans, even me. One of these new theories is called the "slow burn" method: Only two days a week for about 20 minutes each day. I kind of like the basic principle, doing all your exercise slowly, deliberately, and intensely, but again it depends upon what you want as your end result. What is it that we want out of our exercise program? What we are striving for is to provide the proper amount of exercise that is genetically required by our bodies in order to live a longer, happier, healthier life. Always remember that we are only after one thing in this book: the basic requirements necessary in order to maintain homeostasis and health. No more and no less. Two days a week for 20 minutes is simply not enough for most people. This may be o.k. once you are already in very good physical condition, both physically and cardio-vascularly. But almost all of us need more, especially if you are just starting an exercise program.

See, one of the other problems is that we have become so out of shape, and at the same time so sick and toxic with "disease," that not everyone is able to do the exact same exercise at the exact same level, right from the start. Until you condition yourself properly to do all the exercise that is necessary for optimum health, you must first find the beginner and then the intermediate levels of exercise that your body can tolerate without injury. Only then can you be placed in the same pot of soup and stirred in with the rest of the people who are already fit. This is where most gyms and exercise books fail. Most of America simply cannot start out doing what they say to do. Believe it or not, you local commercial gym may be the worst place to start, because there is only one right way, and many wrong ways to use the weights and advanced machines in those gyms. Most gym memberships include a quick tour and a 15-minute crash course in the use of the equipment, and then you are on your own. I can't tell you how many people I have treated in my practice who came in with injuries suffered in the local commercial gym. Many of the proprietors of these gyms, and even many of the athletic trainers they hire, got the same 15-minute crash course that they give you when you join them. A proper course in athletic training takes more than a year to complete. Some certifications take as much as three years. Before joining a local commercial gym, please check the references of the athletic trainers, and then sign up for at least a few personal training sessions, mostly to become familiar with the proper use of the equipment in the facility. But before you even do that, you pretty much need to be in fair shape before you go. Few of these places emphasize the very basics of exercise for beginners, including proper stretching before *and after* an exercise session.

Also, many people have a variety of physical conditions that necessitate evaluation by a health-care professional who is well versed in exercise physiology, like a Subluxation-Based Wellness-Chiropractor, or a sports-medicine doctor. Then they need a specific customized program to start with, one that will not negatively affect their special physical condition or health concern.

Then they can slowly make the transition to a full exercise program. Please consult a certified wellness expert first if you have any specific health concerns, or are obese, or treating for a specific disease condition.

About stretching:

Proper stretching before and after strenuous exercise is essential for the beginner, and for the very advanced athlete who already has very well-developed muscles and a high fitness level, and performs in sports that require fast, explosive muscle contraction and or extreme body positions. For the intermediate-level athlete, and the average person who exercises regularly and is already in fair physical condition, stretching becomes less important, although still a good idea. But for those on the two extreme ends of the scale, stretching is the key ingredient in preventing injuries and in preparing your body for strenuous exercise.

What does the scientific research say about why we should stretch?

Stretching relaxes your mind. It does this by reducing muscle tension, making your body feel more relaxed, but also the muscle activity itself produces chemicals that promote overall relaxation in your body and mind.

Stretching allows for freer and easier movement and so aids in coordination.

Stretching increases range of motion in muscle and in joints.

Stretching helps prevent injury.

Stretching helps prepare your muscle for strenuous activity by increasing blood flow and signaling a muscle that it is about to be used.

Stretching develops body awareness.

Stretching connects your mind to your body for better control of movement, aiding reflexes, and better balance.

Stretching promotes general circulation.

Stretching feels good.

There is a right way and a wrong way to stretch. The right way is to be relaxed and comfortable. You should focus on the muscle being stretched, and sustain the stretch without "bouncing." The wrong way, practiced by most people, is to "bounce" or push up and down to get a further stretch. Also wrong is to stretch to the point of significant pain. Remember, pain is a sign that something is wrong, always. If you stretch correctly, that is, for a few minutes every 12 hours, every day, you will soon see that every body movement you make becomes easier. That's once in the morning for a few minutes, and then once in the evening for a few minutes, seven days a week. It should be part of your daily routine like brushing your teeth.

You should start by doing what is called the easy stretch, for about 10-30 seconds. This is stretching the muscle to the point of just feeling light mild tension. Then relax and hold that position with no bouncing, with no movement at all. The feeling of tension should subside as you hold this position. If it doesn't, ease off a bit because you are stretching too far. You should do this for your arms, legs, neck and back. Then you are ready for a deeper stretch, sometimes called the "developmental stretch." After the easy stretch, just move slowly into the developmental stretch until you feel a little more tension in the muscle group, and then hold it for 10-30 seconds. Doing the easy stretch then the deeper stretch in succession, every day, will actually lengthen and relax the muscle and make it more flexible and less prone to injury.

While stretching, it is very important to relax and breathe. Breathing should be slow and controlled. Never hold your breath. No stretch should ever impede your natural breathing. If it does, then back off a little, or change your position so that you can breathe easily. Remember to stay relaxed. Try to stretch all your muscles equally. In the beginning you may notice that some muscle groups are tighter on one side of your body than the other. In that case you can stretch the tighter side a little more or a little longer until they catch up with the other side. If a consistent inequality persists from side to side, consult your chiropractor, as you may have a joint restriction problem that needs to be specifically corrected by a professional.

You should also know about the "stretch reflex":

Your muscles and tendons are innately protected by your nervous system by something called the "stretch reflex." Any time a muscle feels like it's being stretched too far, a nerve reflex responds to the over-stretch, and sends a signal to the muscle to contract. This keeps your muscle from stretching to the point that it might tear apart. But this reflex makes the muscle tighter, not looser. So when you stretch too far, or try to bounce slightly up and down to go farther, you actually tighten the very muscle you are trying to stretch! Stretching harder is actually counter productive. This is a basic scientific fact of muscle physiology. Yet every day in gyms across America, you see supposedly expert athletic trainers, trying to get their clients to get that extra stretch, and even forcing it by putting their hands on the person stretching, and giving a little push of their own. I also see this in karate dojos (gyms) that I visit all the time. I even see it being done by physical therapists trying to help a patient recover from an injury or surgery. Taking a limb and forcing it to stretch beyond what is comfortable is always counterproductive and does more harm than good. "No pain, no gain" is just plain wrong when it comes to stretching a muscle, especially when it is by a physical therapist trying to rehabilitate someone from a back injury, something I have seen first hand in my practice regularly, for many years. Bouncing, causing the stretch reflex, causes direct damage to the muscle and tendon, resulting in microscopic tears that actually now pre-dispose the muscle to even further injury. This tearing can lead to scar tissue and eventual loss of elasticity. Then the muscle becomes more tight and sore, prompting the physical therapist, athletic trainer, or karate instructor to stretch it even harder. Please learn to pay attention to your body. Pain is always a sign that something is wrong, and you should stop doing whatever is causing the pain.

The great thing about stretching is that it can be done at almost any time and almost anywhere. You don't need a special place like a gym. It is important to stretch before *and after* any strenuous physical activity, if you are a beginner, or if you are an advanced athlete competing in a strenuous sport. If you are in good shape and are used to regular exercise, you could get away with stretching only before your exercise session, but you should also stretch for a few minutes each morning and evening, to start and end the day. This is in addition to your pre- and post-exercise stretch, which means you may be stretching as much as four times per day. You can also stretch at work to relieve tension. You should stretch after sitting too long, especially after a long drive if you feel stiff when you get out of the car. Please get into a daily stretching routine for at least five to six minutes every morning and again every evening. This is a minimum requirement for health.

Stretching is o.k., but what about that "other" exercise; you know, the kind most Americans hate? Well, all I can say about that is, learn not to hate it. Hate is negative and can cause stress, which can cause illness. Love exercise; you will get a lot more health benefits out of it if you do. You don't have to love the "working out at the gym with weights" kind of exercise like a body-builder. I don't like that very much myself. But if you do like it a lot, then go ahead; don't stop.

There are literally hundreds of things you can do to exercise your body that do not involve going to a gym and lifting weights. Not that I'm putting that down. Weight training or "resistance training" has loads of benefits. If done slow and controlled, with the proper lifting technique, weight training alone could provide you with most, if not all of the benefits you may need for proper healthy exercise. But if you really don't like it at first, then I suggest you find something that you do like so that it is not a burden for you to do. Play a sport. Basketball at the park, or on a team. Tennis. Rollerblade. Running, jogging, bicycle-riding, hiking, anything. Something that is strenuous that you can work up a sweat doing, if you really tried. You have to like it a little, because you have to do it a lot. Again, the key is consistency. Hiking is great, but not if you only do it once a week or less. And hiking does not really exercise ALL your muscles in the proper amounts needed. Find something else to do, in addition, that you can do about every other day, four days a week. Find a gym that has a pool. Swimming is one of the best all-around exercises there is. If weights bore you, then there are plenty of gyms with pools, racquetball courts, tennis courts, basketball gyms, indoor tracks, spin classes, aerobic and dance classes, and other fun things to do. Join a karate school. Join a yoga class. There is something for everyone if you just look around. Or stay home and use that wasted space in your basement or garage. But I do recommend finding a partner, a family member, or a group to do it with you. This keeps you motivated, and keeps you from getting bored.

There are two main types of exercise: aerobic and anaerobic exercise. Aerobic exercise includes things that get your heart rate up enough to exercise your heart. Running, jogging, spin classes, step classes, cycling, rowing, the list is endless. Again, find something that you like to do that will work up a little sweat. Anaerobic exercises have been classified as weight-resistant exercises or strength training. But recent research shows that these typical "gym workout" exercises can also benefit your cardiovascular system as well. A great gym workout would consist of about 25 minutes on a treadmill, elliptical, or stationary bike, followed by about 25 minutes of a diversified weight training program, done very slowly and precisely. That's it; every other day, four days a week, is all you may need to get healthy and stay healthy. You don't have to spend hours in a gym with a personal trainer to get the benefits. In fact, buying a few pieces of equipment and doing it in your basement or garage will save you time, and in the long run, a lot of money.

But there are two main problems with home exercise. One is that you have to stay motivated to do it consistently. I see too many exercise machines ending up being used as clothes hangers, or worse. The other problem is that you have to learn how to use the equipment correctly so you don't injure yourself. Depending on the shape of your spine and your overall conditioning level, this will be different for different people. So if you go this route, you want to consult a Subluxation-Based Wellness-Chiropractor who is familiar with exercise physiology and can examine your spine first, before you start an intensive program.

Of all the thousands of books written about health, wellness, and exercise, I have come across very few that really explain to you in detail how to lift weights properly, and how to use the many complicated machines that you find in newer modern gyms these days. Find an expert athletic trainer and take just a few sessions to learn the how-to before you do it on your own. Unfortunately, this is my best advice if you are going to go the weight-lifting route. Once you have learned the basics well, then just eliminate the "dead-lifts" and "squats with weight on your shoulders" that they may have taught you, since these two exercise are never absolutely necessary, and always absolutely dangerous to do, especially if you are by yourself. Also, eliminate any weight-bearing exercise that puts a weighted bar across your shoulders behind your neck. This is always improper technique and always dangerous even if you're shown how to do it correctly, because over time it will slowly do damage to your upper spine and neck.

Always do all your weight resistance exercises very slowly and deliberately, never using a fast motion. It is improper technique and always invites injury. Also, always run away from most of the body-building-no-pain-no-gain muscle-bound gym rats. They may be wonderful people outside the gym, but in 25 years I have never met one who had a healthy spine, a healthy body, or who was not in constant pain from an injury. I apologize for this generalization, but for the hundreds of them that I have met, and the thousands more I have heard about from my colleagues, this has always been true. They confuse fitness and strength for health. They are not the same thing.

A person can be very fit with regard to muscle and body-fat content and still be in poor health, and a person can be very healthy without big muscles. Jack La Lanne is a perfect example. He exercises strenuously everyday at age 90 plus. He never had huge muscles and never took drugs or dangerous supplements. Every serious bodybuilder I have ever met has a health problem, and every one of them dies young. This is mostly due to the crazy diets they use, the overload of supplements, which destroys their kidneys and liver, and of course the steroid use. Even one-time steroid use can damage your body permanently.

Many modern bodybuilders are beginning to shy away from these dangerous drugs, but most still do the many other things that are very unhealthy. Many of them are wonderful people and some of them are very close friends of mine. They are just slightly misguided by their peers and the bodybuilding magazines they read. Remember, those magazines exist only for the purpose of making money and advertising things to sell to make even more money. They do not have any interest in your health. They only have interest in the size of your muscles and the size of their own bank accounts. Don't try to learn how to lift weights properly from a muscle magazine or from most muscle-bound gym rats, although there are a few rare great ones who do know what they are doing.

Please don't go overboard. Balance is the key. Get a consistent and easily doable routine of exercise planned into your weekly schedule.

Fifty to sixty minutes a day, four to five days a week, should be just about right for most people who are interested in better health.

Start your stretching exercises today.

The truth about health is that health comes from moderation and balance in all things, including exercise.

Chapter 10

Putting It All Together... The 5 Keys to Health!

"...where there is peace and meditation there is neither anxiety nor doubt"

You now know the secret formula that is the key to living a longer, happier, healthier life. I call this formula "The Five Keys to Health." I have been teaching this formula in various forms for many years to thousands of people. The five keys to health are:

Proper Functioning Nervous System, or getting your spine checked and working better. (Chapter 6)

De-stressing, sometimes called PMA, for positive mental attitude. (Chapter 5)

Nutrition (chapter 7)

Rest and Sleep (chapter 8)

Exercise (chapter 9)

The last four are up to you. Improved nervous system function is up to your Subluxation-Based Wellness-Chiropractor. Of course the decision to get your spine checked and your nervous system function improved is also ultimately up to you, so you are in total control of all of the five keys to health. You can choose to get as much out of each of them as you want. But, putting my professional license on the line, I will give you a guarantee that few other doctors of any specialty will give you:

If you do all five keys to health together at the same time over a period of time, I *guarantee* that you will have fewer aches and pains, fewer colds and flu, better quality rest and sleep, more energy during the day, higher resistance to disease, and a longer, happier, healthier life!

The five keys to health are a specific formula that works every time! There is no better formula for health. There is no magic pill or potion. The only trick is that you should choose to do all five at the same time. You can't pick and choose one or two and not the others and still expect the optimum results. Remember the plant analogy we made when discussing how drug company studies are done? Remember the pond analogy? If you have ever taken care of a garden, or even just a house plant, you know you can't just put it in the sun and that's all. You know that you can't just water it once in a while and that's all. You can't just give it plant food once in a while and that's all. And you certainly can't clean it with toxic cleaning products and expect it to do well. Your body has exactly the same requirements. You also require food and water and sunlight, and you need to avoid toxins if you want your body to thrive and be truly healthy. So if you do all five keys to health all together at the same time over a period of time, you will get the virtual guarantee of improved health that I stated.

Please don't forget the most important ingredient: mental attitude! Attitude in general and your attitude toward the five keys to health specifically. I have spent a major part of this book teaching you about being positive, setting worthy goals, and keeping positive images in your head at all times to push out the negative. You are much more than just the sum of your parts. Your thoughts, attitudes, and opinions ARE you. If you are a negative, "glass-half-empty" kind of person, then life's stresses will have more of a negative effect on you than the person who is always positive. You will be sicker, and that's a fact, a fact that has been proven many times in the scientific literature. But it goes deeper than that. If you want to be healthier but you hate exercising, hate eating well, and hate going to bed on time, then you will not get the most optimum benefits from doing these things, and you probably won't stick to doing them consistently. When you have a positive mental attitude in general, then your attitude toward nutrition, exercise, and sleeping right will also be more positive. Then you'll get even more benefits from them, as well as sticking to them for a lifetime, translating into a lifetime of better health. Nothing is more important than this concept.

So as far as implementing these new goals for health, you should make the transition and implementation as slow and as gradual, and as positive, as you need to in order to make it easy and permanent. Remember to write your goals down and review and repeat them every day. Set reasonable goals within reasonable timeframes. And be positive when writing your goals. The goal should not be weight loss; the goal is health and well-being. The goal should not be less pain; it should be better function. The goal is not big muscles; it should be fitness and vitality. Never use words like can't, don't, won't, or "have to." These words are associated with negativity and can result in anxiety, pressure, and stress, which are always counterproductive to health. Instead, use the words, "choose," "choice," "can," "will" and "I want to." Try to remember that everything is a choice.

Choose health. The side effects of health are losing weight, performing better, looking better, and feeling great. These will come to you naturally when you decide to make the better health choices we have outlined. This is where all the diet books and exercise books have failed you in the past. They are loaded with stress, pressure, and negativity. They are often associated with denial. They also have too narrow of a focus, like "losing weight" (by eating very <u>unhealthy</u> food that sheds pounds and adds disease) or making big over-pumped muscles (by destroying your liver, kidneys, and heart), and on and on. We are no longer going to think like that. Now we know "why" the health choices in this book are the right thing to do, and so it should be easier to make these choices. Now we "know that we know" these health choices "are" the right thing to do, because we have all the scientific information to back it up, so we can now remove all doubt and anxiety and just get healthy, with confidence, by making these healthy lifestyle choices.

Removing that stress will accelerate your desired results. Now it's just a matter of choosing more and more healthy things, which will slowly push out and replace the unhealthy things that we were doing before. There soon won't be room for both. We will let in so much light that darkness cannot exist anymore. Remember what Dr. James Chestnut said: Sickness and disease are like darkness; they don't really exist. They are just the lack of health. Add more health, and sickness and disease are automatically reduced.

"...But where do I start..." you say?

"Little drops of water wear down big stones."

Take baby steps at first if you have to. Doing everything in this book all at once, starting today, may be overwhelming for some people. For others it is the right way to go about it. It depends on where your head is at right now, as well as where your level of health is. So find out.

We have established how to make lists and write your priorities down, and I have even given you a sample list that you can use to get started. We know that our list will be positive, and maybe even inspirational, but at the same time practical and doable. Many people are resistant to change and need to get their toes wet before jumping in. There is a lot of information in this book, and much of it may be different than what you have been doing for your health or even thinking about your health. That's o.k. Just start with the chapter on stress and write your lists, remembering that positive and worthy ideals are the key. This is where everyone should start their program. This is your first action step in improving your health and your life. We will not focus on what you will not be doing or eating anymore from this point on. We will simply set goals and work toward achieving them logically and scientifically. Focus on what you will be doing to add more health to your life.

Maybe health is really not your number one priority right now. Maybe after you complete your lists and then prioritize them you will find that you have to work on something else first and handle that, before health can move closer to the top of your list. That's fine for now. Just don't wait too long to improve your health because it does affect every other thing in your life. Just take a few easy and simple things from each chapter and try to add them to your days as you go along, taking care of whatever your priority happens to be at the present time. You can always add a little health along the way at any time. Any fruit or vegetable at any time is always better than any fast-food burger, at any time. No matter what else you have to do, you still have to eat at some point in the day. You might as well eat well. So after you make your lists, improving your nutrition is always a good second step.

If you crave a certain favorite food that you know is very unhealthy, then eat it. But only eat it in front of a full length mirror when you are completely naked, keeping in mind what that food is doing to the inside of your body and to your health in general. Then you'll see how long this will remain your favorite food. Even if it does remain a favorite food, I promise you will be eating it a lot less often. This may sound crazy, but I assure you it works. If weight is an issue for you, try eating most of your meals naked in front of a mirror for just a few days. This really works because you are making a visual connection to the consequences of your actions. The more of your senses you involve the better. SEE yourself doing it. HEAR yourself doing it. IMAGINE what is happening to your body as a result of your choices.

Soon vegetables and fruits will become 70% of your meals. Soon exercise won't be an inconvenient chore, but a pleasure, because it makes you feel good. Soon you will be going to bed on time without any effort at all. Soon you will visit a Subluxation-Based Wellness-Chiropractor, and realize the awesome power of your nervous system and what improved brain and nervous system function can do for your health.

Bad habits are hard to break, but once you develop these good habits, they will be hard to break, too. Try picking just two really healthy things to do and stick to doing them for 50 to 100 days in a row. Then pick two more, and then pick two more. Soon you will have some good habits that will also be hard to break.

> *"Motivation is what gets you started. Habit is what keeps you going."*
>
> Jim Ryun

But it all starts with positive attitude, an open mind, and willingness change to the right choices for the right reasons. Start each day with a positive affirmation statement that will help get you going in the morning. I have seen this work wonders for some people. Something like:

"I get better everyday, in everything I do and say."

May sound a little corny, but it will train your brain to start thinking positively, and that's the most important thing you can ever do.

Another great one that I have used myself is:

"I am alive and I am grateful. Today I will do my best to be a better person, for myself, and for others. May I be at peace, may my heart remain open, may I know the beauty of my own true nature, may I be healed."

Here's another good one:

"God, (or life, or Mother Nature, or Mighty Joe, whatever) thank you for this day. Please keep your hand on my shoulder to remind me to do what is right in all things."

Of course if you are an attorney or a drug company executive, you will have to change your profession. (Just kidding; sorry.) But for many people these simple statements can have a profound effect on your mental attitude, your life, and your future. You can use these or make up one of your own, but get in the habit of saying something positive to start every day. Arm yourself with the power of a positive mental attitude. Please don't ever start the day by cursing at the alarm clock, or the deadline you have to meet, or the singing bird outside your window.

You can also arm your self with other tools of the health trade as your budget allows. Here is a short list:

Arm yourself with a water filter, a food processor, a steamer, natural veggie-wash, stainless steel pots and pans, glass containers for all your food, a slow cooker, a good mattress, a small pillow, an alarm clock that wakes you up to music or talk, no buzzer, and all-natural cleaning products.

You can also get a wobble board, an exercise ball, and an exercise mat. I also suggest an elastic band-type exerciser instead of weights if you are going to do most of your exercise at home.

Do some house cleaning; get rid of these items:

Teflon/non-stick pans, plastic containers for food, microwave ovens, chemical cleaners like bleach, Windex, and Tide. Also, chemical hair dyes, makeup, antiperspirant, nail polish, fluoride toothpastes, commercial shampoo and soaps, most skin creams and lotions. Sorry, ladies, I know this sounds tough, if not impossible. Remember that your skin absorbs these chemicals into your body, so if you would not eat it or drink it, then don't put it on your skin. I know this is a very tough one for most women. It is still a fact that these things are toxic and are killing you. I've done the research and I can tell you for sure that these things are a lot more deadly than you think they are and never worth having or doing for any reason. Please don't kill the messenger; I'm only reporting the facts. Just remember: If it was not available to use 5,000 years ago or more, then you probably should not be using it today.

Of course, I'm not forcing you to stop using all these products, it's always your choice. All I can promise is that not only won't you be as healthy as you can be if you continue to use them, but it is a fact that most of them are actually causing you to be sick in many cases. Try using an all-natural organic coconut oil for all your skin care needs. I promise you will be happy with the results. Like I said, just try it for about 100 days in a row, then go back and see the difference.

After you have your lists going, make another list... a shopping list. Start with a few healthy nutritional choices and experiment with some recipes. After your priority lists, this is always a good second step in the program, like I said previously, because you see and feel the effects in a short period of time, and because you have to eat anyway, no matter what else is going on in your life.

The next step is to start with some daily stretching exercises and maybe some long-distance walking if you have the time. This is the best third step toward a healthier lifestyle. Remember it is a required ingredient for health. A little more exercise in combination with a little more healthy food will work wonders and keep you motivated. You'll feel better right away and want to do the other keys to health as outlined.

Next, you should start working on your sleep routine. Make small easy changes that you can stick to without much effort. Get rid of that buzzer, and wake up at the same exact time each day to something pleasant-sounding. Slowly add the other keys to better sleep that I have outlined. Once you train your brain to control your sleep pattern, you will be revitalized like never before.

Of course, I strongly recommend that you make a bunch of phone calls and find yourself a Subluxation-Based Wellness-Chiropractor who is well versed in nutrition and exercise. Get your spine checked for subluxations. If it is confirmed that you have subluxation of your spine, have them reduced or corrected as soon as possible, and keep them corrected as long as possible. This literally saved my life, and it could save your life too. At least give it a try.

Be sure to ask the doctor these questions:

Do you use a specific technique to adjust spines?

Do you adjust all spinal areas?

Do you take x-rays in your office if you suspect a problem?

Are you a subluxation-based doctor?

Do you provide wellness care for entire families?

Do you provide general nutritional and exercise advice? (Be careful if they sell supplements out of their office.... Remember what we said about agendas...)

Get a "yes" to these basic questions. Then ask him about your condition if you have one, and what is his or her success rate with that condition. Remember, if he says he only treats subluxations in your spine and does nothing else to treat "conditions", that's not a bad thing. In fact, it may be great. You have all the other information you need, anyway, right here in this book. Just remember that not all chiropractors are the same.

If you are still not sure then feel free to contact my office. I have referral list of chiropractors in almost every state.

Once you get started with these five keys to health, it would be a good idea to read this book again, taking notes on the information you need to know that you did not remember the first time. Then do a little further investigation on topics that interest you or that you want to know more about.

...Chapter 10-b...

(Is that all there is?)

"People have a hard time letting go of their suffering. Out of fear of the unknown they prefer suffering, that is familiar."

Thich Nhat Hanh

Yes, for now that's all there is.

Sure I could fill a book on almost any one of the chapters already presented. Perhaps someday I will. But I think this is a great start. The information presented so far is enough to give you the guarantee of improved health that I mentioned earlier. I don't want to bore some of you with lots of details that not every reader may be interested in. However, every reader needs to know the basics that I have already presented here. If you are interested in one of the topics and want more information about it, then you should read some of the scientific references listed at the back.

I have presented to you the essential basics for health that everyone should know. I know them all to be true based on the current available scientific research, and by the fact that I have seen these principles work in my practice. In fact, they have never failed. You need only to implement them. But for the last time, please don't make them become "work" or a "chore." Don't associate anything you do with anything negative, especially with any of the five keys to health. Approach each one with that positive mental attitude we have talked so much about.

I hope you have learned something that will help you on your journey toward health. If nothing else, you are now armed with true scientific health information that you can use to confront anyone out there who may say something different. Not just family and friends, but even your medical doctor, so this information can very easily save your life.

Hopefully you will do more than that. I sincerely wish that you will <u>use the information on a daily basis,</u> and in a practical way, to get healthy, healthier than you have ever been before. I want you to teach everyone what you learned in this book, but the best way to teach is to lead by example. Become healthy using these methods. Do it with joy and love. Do it with an open mind and an open heart. Do it because it is the right thing to do. You won't have to preach the benefits to others. Others will want to follow in your footsteps.

> *"You must be the change you wish to see in the world."*
>
> *Gandhi*

I will leave you with these final quotes:

> *"...And then the day came when the risk to remain tight in a bud was more painful than the risk to bloom."*
>
> *Anais Nin*

This is you. Let go of your past. Live in the present and future only. Be the blossoming bud.

> *"My interest is only in the future, because I am going to spend the rest of my life there."*

> *"Between saying and doing, many a pair of shoes has been worn out."*
>
> *Italian Proverb*

It's great to finally know the truth about health, but knowledge is power only if you use it. Truth without action is a waste of your knowledge. It may be long and hard, but the journey is well worth it.

> *"You have never really lived until you have done something for somebody who can never repay you."*

A true statement, and one of the reasons I wrote the book. Finally, and most importantly...

> **"A Master in the art of living makes no distinction between his work and his play,**
>
> **His labor and his leisure,**
>
> **His mind and his body,**
>
> **His education and his recreation,**
>
> **His love and his religion.**
>
> **He hardly knows which is which.**
>
> **He simply pursues a vision of excellence in whatever he does,**

Leaving others to decide whether he is working or playing.

To him he is always doing both."

Buddha

Pursue excellence in health; it is a game well worth playing.

References, Bibliography, and Further Recommended Reading:

MILK, The Deadly Poison. Robert Cohen: Argus Publishing, Inc. 1998

"Training the Mind, Healing The Body," Deepak Chopra M.D., David Simon, M.D.

The Book of Secrets. Deepak Chopra, M.D.

Journey to the Boundless. Deepak Chopra, M.D.

"Innate physical fitness and spinal hygiene." James L. Chestnut B.Ed., Msc., D.C. (contains more that 50 references to peer-reviewed scientific medical journals)

"The Innate State of Mind." James L. Chestnut B.Ed., Msc., D.C. (contains more that 50 references to peer-reviewed scientific medical journals)

"The 14 Foundational Premises for the Scientific and Philosophical Validation of The Chiropractic Wellness Paradigm." James L. Chestnut B.Ed., Msc., D.C. (contains more that 75 references to peer-reviewed scientific medical journals)

"The Innate Diet and Natural Hygiene." James L. Chestnut B.Ed., Msc., D.C. (contains more that 50 references to peer-reviewed scientific medical journals)

The Sanctity of Human Blood. Tim O'Shea. 8th edition, 2004 (This is a must-read for everyone who has children or plans to have children.)

Know Your Nutrition. Linda A. Clark, Nutritionist

The Complete Encyclopedia of Natural Healing. Gary Null, Ph.D.

The Nutrition Almanac. John D. Kirschmann

Prescription for Nutritional Healing. Third edition. Phyllis A. Balch, CNC (This is a great reference book to keep around the house for emergencies. Tons of good info.)

Obstetrics Illustrated. Garrey, Govan, Hodge, Callander, M.D.'s

Synopsis of Pediatrics. James G. Hughes, M.D.

Chiropractic First. Terry A. Rondberg, D.C.

Chiropractic Textbook. R.W. Stephenson, D.C, Ph.C.

Gray's Anatomy. Warwick and Williams. W.B. Saunders Company. 35th Edition

"Somatovisceral Aspects of Chiropractic, An Evidence-based Approach," Dr. Charles S. Masarsky, Dr.Marion T. Masarsky. (clinical and scientific evidence on the whole-body implications of chiropractic care)

Food Politics: How the Food Industry Influences Nutrition and Health. Marion Nestle.

Evidence of Harm. David Kirby (another must-read if you have children)

The Stresses of Life. Hans Selye, M.D.

Stress without Distress. Hans Selye, M.D. 1974

Patient, Heal Thyself. Jordan S. Rubin, N.M.D., C.N.C.

"Bovine Somatotropin Supplementation of Dairy Cows. Is the Milk Safe?" *JAMA.* 264(8) August 22, 1990

Fit for Life. Harvey and Marilyn Diamond. Warner Communications. 1994

"Subluxation-Based Research." Boone, W. *JVSR.* 1998. 2(4): 173-174

Wolfe MM, Lichtenstein Dr., "Gastrointestinal Toxicity of Non-steroidal Anti-inflammatory Drugs." *NEJM.* 1999. 340

HY Son, A. Nishikawa, T. Ikeda, T. Imazawa, S. Kimura, and M. Hirose "Lack of effect of soy isoflavone on thyroid hyperplasia." *Japan J Cancer Res.* 2001. 92:103-108

Sharpe R.M., Martin B., Morris K., Greig I., McKinnell C., McNeilly A.S., Walker M., "Infant feeding with soy formula milk; effects on the testis and on blood testosterone levels during neonatal testicular activity." *Hum Report.* 2002. July. 17:7

www.soyonlineservice.com.nz.

Today's Chiropractic. New South Publishing, 1303 Hightower Trail, Atlanta GA 2005

Koren Publications Inc., Ted Koren, D.C., Koren. korenpublications.com

Mayo Clinic Health Letter. March 2000. Vol. 18

Cailliet, Renee M.D. *Low Back Pain Syndrome.* Philadelphia: FA Davis Co. 1981

Feingold, BF. *Why Is Your Child Hyperactive?* New York: Random House, Inc. 1975

Giesen, J.M., Center, D.B. and Leach, R.A. "An Evaluation of Chiropractic Manipulation as Treatment of Hyperactivity in Children." *Journal of Manipulation and Physiological Therapeutics.* October 1989. 12

Ostgood, M.D., Anderson, M.D. Shultz, PhD, Miller, Ph.D. "Influence of biomechanical factors on low back pain in pregnancy." *Spine Magazine.* Vol. 18. 1993

Rothman, M.D., Simone, M.D. *The Spine.* 3rd edition. W.B. Saunders. 1992

Levin, M. M.D. "U.S. won't alert parents, doctors of mercury in flu shots." *Los Angeles Times.* 2 April, 2004

Recognize The Grain Danger! Shari Lieberman, Ph.D., CNS, FACN. CE-2007

"Nutritional Supplements, Physician Grade vs. OTC." John V. Wood. CE-2007

Fateful Harvest. Duff Wilson. (PLEASE READ THIS BOOK)

For more information, contact:
Elite Family Wellness Center
Dr. Bill F. Puglisi, D.C., C.C.W.P.
195 Route 46 West, Suite 8
Totowa, NJ 07512

"The Beginning"

About the Author:

Dr. Bill F. Puglisi, D.C., C.C.W.P., graduated from Palmer College of Chiropractic in Iowa, in 1982, as an honors student, and as a National Board Diplomat. Since then he has maintained a natural health care practice, and continued his research into wellness. His continuing education in the field of natural health, including many advanced courses in nutrition, exercise physiology, and many other specific natural health care techniques, have combined to make him a unique expert in the field of Holistic Wellness Care. He has been a member of the I.C.A., A.C.A., N.J.C.S, A.N.J.C., The Health- Awareness Foundation, The Wellness Education foundation, The Professional Chiropractic Society of America, The Holistic Moms Network, and was on the Board of Recreation Advisory Council of the City of Paterson, N.J. as well as the Paterson Community civic Organization, Inc. He has been a part of many other local and national health-related organizations over the past 25 years.

He was a teaching assistant at Upsala College in New Jersey, and at Palmer College in Iowa. He was also head of the Five-Points Chiropractic Intern Program in Davenport Iowa, which was part of the Gonstead Advanced Technique Seminars program. He is also listed in the Metropolitan Executive and Professional Registry, as well as the Global Who's Who registry. Dr. Puglisi has been fully certified as a specific Wellness Practitioner by the International Chiropractic Association Counsel on Wellness Science. He is one of only a handful of doctors in the entire country to achieve this status.

Dr. Puglisi has achieved an unmatched success rate with his patients, which speaks for itself.

Now he is sharing his complete health care system with you. In this concise, easy to read, how-to book on Wellness Care, he reveals the bottom line on how to get healthy and stay healthy for life. What sets this book apart from others is the very specific and scientific documentation of his work, which leaves no room for doubt about the information he presents. This book is a "must-read" for anyone interested in improving their health in a real and natural way.

Printed in the United States
201901BV00002B/304-519/P